VITAL SIGNS 3

Restructuring the English Classroom

Edited by
James L. Collins
State University of New York
at Buffalo

Boynton/Cook Publishers
Heinemann
Portsmouth, NH

Boynton/Cook Publishers, Inc.
A Subsidiary of
Heinemann Educational Books, Inc.
361 Hanover Street, Portsmouth, NH 03801–3959
Offices and agents throughout the world

The following have generously given permission to use quotations from
copyrighted works:

Page 17: "Traveling at Home" from COLLECTED POEMS, 1957–1982,
copyright © 1984 by Wendell Berry. Published by North Point Press and
reprinted by permission.
Page 76: "961-Baby" by Dora Simpson. From *Corridors: Stories from
Inner-city Detroit*. Edited by David Schaafsma. Ann Arbor: Center for
Educational Improvement Through Collaboration, 1986.

Every effort has been made to contact the copyright holders and students
for permission to reprint borrowed material. We regret any oversights that
may have occurred and would be happy to rectify them in future
printings of this work.

ISBN 0-86709-297-1
ISSN 1045-2672

Printed in the United States of America
92 93 94 95   10 9 8 7 6 5 4 3 2 1

Contents

Introduction

*R*estructuring means change. We hear a lot these days about educational change, about reforming schools, empowering teachers, making students responsible for their own learning, creating multicultural curricula, teaching critical thinking, using technology and more. Rarely in this discussion, however, do we hear the voices of teachers. This volume of *Vital Signs* aims to change that.

Vital Signs 3 is about change and who should control it. Contributors tell about reconfiguring and redefining the teaching and learning of English, and they tell us classroom teachers should be doing the reconfiguring and redefining. They identify the inner qualities and abilities possessed by teachers who make change a positive force, and they explore the characteristics of curricula and classrooms where diverse and significant changes have been implemented, changes such as teaching for multiple intelligences and differing abilities; taking on issues of class, race, gender, and sexuality; using discussion and technology; and updating teacher education.

Throughout the volume contributors stand opposed to the conventional "top-down" model of educational restructuring. This model presents a vertical metaphor for change; "top-down" refers to the fact that control over restructuring flows from administrators to teachers. In my capacity as director of a small project that reviews educational software, I receive a steady stream of mail intended for school administrators, and it all favors the top-down model. One brochure recently advertised a conference called "Peak Performance for Educators." The conference takes place in Denver and the brochure shows tall buildings with mountains in the background, suggesting the vertical metaphor again. Peak performance is for people in high places. The brochure promises to show how to "help ordinary people achieve extraordinary results" and how to "restructure your school to promote peak performance."

In contrast to the top-down model of restructuring, contributors to *Vital Signs 3* advocate an active role for teachers. To see what they mean, try taking the word "reform" and inserting a hyphen: re-form. With that small change educational reform stops being an entity and becomes a process. It stops being something imposed on teachers and becomes a way teachers relate to their work, to their students, and to one another. Re-forming is shaping again, exerting control over change. Restructuring means change, but it also means taking charge of change.

Part One is about why the restructuring of English curricula and classrooms is necessary and about why the work of restructuring should be done by teachers. Susan Ohanian's chapter discusses an inner dimension of structure, a strength from within, a source of teachers' trust in themselves and their own designs. Restructuring begins with nurturing the inner self and building our own foundations, since "everything about this insecure calling we call teaching teases and tempts us to tack on one more addition from somebody else's floorplan." Ohanian prods us to accept change as constant and desirable and to accept for ourselves the same qualities we would have for our students: self-discovery, confidence, patience, and faith in risk-taking and diversity. This dimension of structure is what helps people make their own choices, and it resides within, resisting the external trappings of educational control such as core reading lists, standard lessons presented to produce fixed outcomes, and curriculum guides telling us what to teach.

If we're going to have restructuring, and Martha West's chapter says most of us are, then we need to make sure it's not just a new set of rules. West claims restructuring isn't accomplished once and for all, or once every generation or so. It's something we do daily, even hourly, as we go about enhancing opportunities for learning by constantly adjusting environments and conditions for learning. West describes restructuring as an interaction between curriculum and teachers' improvisations. "Improvisational teaching means putting together our prior knowledge and experience with the daily revisions of our work," and it results from teachers trusting their own intuition, imagination, and internalized expertise.

Part Two presents methods for restructuring English classrooms. Peter Smagorinsky's chapter proposes that we provide students with alternatives to the primary activities of expression and response, not to replace those activities but to supplement them. Schools favor two modes of intelligence, the linguistic and logical/mathematical modes, and Smagorinsky advocates including five other modes: musical, spatial, bodily, interpersonal, and intrapersonal. He describes these additional modes of intelligent behavior and then shows how teachers can structure classrooms so students can express themselves through unconventional intelligences; examples include interviews to use interpersonal intelligence, videos and computer presentations to use spatial intelligence, and journals to provide an outlet for intrapersonal intelligence. Other chapters in the volume recommend related strategies, such as Sharon Thomas on drawing to show relatedness among ideas, Denise David on double-entry journals to connect reading and response, and Bob Beichner, Jim Collins, and Susan Szymanski on mapmaking as a bridge between science and writing.

Suzanne Miller interviewed students about their roles in class discussions, and her chapter reveals how teachers can help students learn new discussion behaviors. The main idea is to have discussion serve the construction of knowledge by matching personal experience with ideas newly encountered through reading. "Because rival possibilities are at issue, students examine the personal and textual bases of their responses, provide and provoke evidence and explanation, challenge with new possibilities." The teacher's purpose is to have students use personal language to explore their thinking by voicing it, and the teacher's role in discussion is an active one — modeling response, redefining roles, "reading" and encouraging students.

Diane Brunner's chapter is about breaking down cultural stereotypes. She begins with an autobiographical account of her struggle against socioeconomic discrimination and its educational counterpart, tracking. Schools sanction attitudes, behaviors, and lifestyles, either by neglect or by conscious attention to moral sensibilities, and Brunner advocates conscious attention in the form of a "course or unit on cultural stereotypes celebrat[ing] diversity by providing experiences that help students become aware of the pervasiveness of sexism, racism, homophobia, ablebodiedness, and stereotypes aimed at Native Americans and international cultures." Brunner describes such an English course and approaches to teaching it.

Among the points Brunner makes is the idea that storytelling can be a powerful means for discovering who we are and how we stand in relation to others. In the next chapter, David Schaafsma and Michael Smith describe how storytelling, especially autobiography, can help students develop authority in writing and reading. They illustrate the connection between autobiography and authority first with a fifth-grader's moving writing about teen pregnancies she's witnessed and then with a teaching method that has students write their own experiences in preparation for reading literary works. They also clarify the value of autobiography. Personal narratives help students learn in school by connecting experience and meaning, and narrative also provides a means for the cultures of community and home to intersect with the culture of schools.

Carolyn Handa's chapter surveys the changes in English teaching brought about by technology, especially by computers in composition classrooms. She organizes the chapter around three terms from the subtitle of *Vital Signs 3*—structure, class, and room—and shows how computers and computer networks are helping to bring about changes in those three. Handa envisions, for example, a paperless composition classroom where all composing, conferencing, revising, and evaluating are done electronically, and she explores the meaning of such a classroom for the ways writers and readers relate to text and to one another.

Part Three is primarily about restructuring teaching and learning in college composition and literature classrooms, but all of the chapters in this section have clear implications for middle schools and high schools as well. Deborah Mutnick's chapter describes a new reading and writing program for underprepared college students. The course is meant to supplant courses that separate reading and writing to provide remediation through skills-oriented practice. The program is built around themes situating students in history and emphasizes social, dialogic interaction among students, teachers, writers, and readers. The program is two semesters long; students begin to develop authority one semester and exercise their authority the next. Readers familiar with the University of Pittsburgh program for basic writers, described in Bartholomae and Petrosky's *Facts, Artifacts, and Counterfacts: Theory and Method for a Reading and Writing Course*, will find useful additions to their ideas in Mutnick's chapter.

The next two chapters also advocate the re-integration of reading and writing, and they extend the concern for helping underprepared college students. Sharon Thomas describes strategies for helping basic writers learn to make reading work for them. Thomas acknowledges the influence of elementary school teachers in her approach, especially those teachers who use whole language and illustration as means of engaging students in the reading-for-learning process. As I mentioned earlier, this chapter uses one of the modes of alternative intelligence in Smagorinsky, namely the visualization of entities and relations. Denise David's chapter describes the use of double-entry journals to help students construct meaningful responses to literature and to reconstruct their responses by comparing them with the text and with other responses. David's students learn to make their own meanings, but they also learn to discern what makes academically acceptable meanings and what does not. "Meaning occurs first at a personal level, but like adjusting the lens of a camera we are able to see more and more of the picture as we share our meanings with others and negotiate these meanings with the actual texts."

Harriet Malinowitz believes our educational system can no longer avoid confronting our society's deepest prejudice. Her chapter places gay and lesbian issues right alongside gender, race, class, and other issues comprising a multicultural curriculum. She covers the kinds of discussions that come up in classes around gay and lesbian issues and tells what she has seen happen in students' writing when they try, from varying perspectives, to compose on so charged a topic. Malinowitz also provides texts and resources available for adoption and experimentation by instructors interested in multicultural pedagogy. There has been a lot of debate lately about whether politically charged social issues belong in writing classes, and Malinowitz has an answer: "The argument at its surface level has been about whether or not ideology belongs in a writing class; at a deeper level, it is about *which* ideology belongs in a writing class, since new historicists, deconstructionists, and social constructivists have shown that culture is never neutral, unmediated, or value-free. Academicians who resisted ideology just at the moment when it ceased to be white and male were really fighting not just academic but vast social and political change."

Part Four is about restructuring teacher education. The chapter by Beichner, Collins, and Symanski describes a course combining a graduate seminar for teachers with a science class for Native American middle school students. Each teacher formed a working partnership with one or two children, and activities ranged from purposeful walks in the woods to writing at computers. The chapter tells what happens when teachers and students learn cooperatively, sharing experiences and sharing processes of learning from experience. It also explores the consequences of restructuring teacher education, especially regarding participatory modes of learning, writing to learn, and teaching writing by co-authoring with students.

Sally Hudson-Ross took very seriously my request to include teachers' voices in her report of teachers' experiences with restructuring. Her chapter is a collection of letters written by fourteen teachers reporting their experiences with turning their classrooms into reading and writing workshops. The letters comprise a conversation, reflecting the cooperative, social nature of this approach to teacher education. Perhaps more than the other chapters, the teachers' letters show us that traditional structures don't just disappear when new ones are adopted;

rather, the traditional forms sometimes co-exist alongside the new and sometimes evolve to accommodate the new forms.

The final chapter by Ruth Vinz searches for what is genuine and central in educational reform. Vinz accuses reform literature of being "technocratic and functionalist, assuming teaching to be a series of acontextualized procedures performed upon learners" and threatening to render teachers voiceless by a "cacophony of outsiders' reform slogans and recipes for improvement." By what means, however, should teachers gather trust in themselves and their own reform designs? Vinz describes four sources: teacher as archeologist, teacher as anthropologist, teacher as artist, and teacher as reformer. The teacher as archeologist constructs knowledge of our history, the narrative of education, and knowledge of the curriculum as artifact, to take a stand on what curriculum is and can be. The teacher as anthropologist studies the increasingly pluralistic cultures of schools to increase the volume of voices from within classrooms and to resist control from cultures outside schools. The teacher as artist is part of a shaping, constructing enterprise, balancing format and freedom, external forces and inner possibilities. The teacher as reformer claims a role, an insider's active and informed role, in an ongoing dialogue over the form and function of education.

What understanding of restructuring emerges from this volume? Certainly an understanding that occupies more of a moral position than a revolutionary one. Contributors use terms like "destructuring" and "unstructuring" occasionally, but more in the sense of loosening up existing structures than in tearing them down. There is no mention, furthermore, of turning things upside down, of replacing the top-down model with a bottom-up one. Given a chance to have their voices heard on matters of educational change, teachers reveal a preference for change from within, guided by qualities of mind and character, moral qualities. Their perspective sees change in English classrooms as resulting from a constant struggle against social inequities and tyrannies of convention and ideology rather than from any once-and-for-all, pre-packaged remedy. If this seems a definition of reform consisting first of a change of spirit followed by a change of structure, such is the nature of change from within.

J. L. C.
University at Buffalo

Part One
MOTIVES

One day I saw the emerging human spirit, the next day the naturalist's dreary landscape. Both were true. And, I guess, this was a tension the children felt, in their way— something they couldn't articulate, perhaps, as I couldn't when I was a child, but they were living it, absorbing it into their marrow.

—*Mike Rose*

Inside Classroom Structures

Susan Ohanian

*I*n order to get an emergency teaching license in New York City
twenty-five years ago, I had to take an education methods course in
which the professor demonstrated how to pass out paper. At first I
thought it was a joke. Not being experienced in educationese, I was
not aware that professors of education did not kid around. Insisting
that this paper-parceling was the make-or-break principle on which a
new teacher's success might well rest, the good professor became
upset when he discovered that not only were some of us in the back of
the room giggling, we had moved our chairs out of alignment. Muttering
about the need for straight rows, he insisted that we get in line so he
could proceed with his demonstration.

Only a person who has never taken a methods course would ask, as
did my husband, if that story is true. Not only is it true, it's not even
my best teacher-training story. At that same college a professor would
not dismiss his class when a fire alarm went off because (1) he didn't
smell smoke and (2) the class was taking an exam and he was afraid he
couldn't control collusion if he let them out of the room. Anyway, I
don't know how to write fiction: the great thing about education
commentary is that you never have to make anything up.

I confess that although I am meticulous about fire alarms in my own
career, I've never been much good at efficiency: paper distribution and
record keeping and time-on-task have pretty much eluded me for the
past twenty-odd years. Nonetheless, when I say I'm not a straight-row
teacher, I'm not talking about where I put the chairs. I've taught
where student desks were bolted down in neat and tidy rows and I've
taught where the students and I bought a big red velvet sofa at the
Salvation Army store. It matters not; I don't measure my worth by how

many times I get the kids sitting in a circle. William Blake reminds us, "A fool sees not the same tree that a wise man sees." No place is this more true than in the classroom. One of the most retrogressive principals I know harangues teachers she catches sitting at their desks, as though being on your feet were equivalent to being on your toes. Classroom structures that really count are internal, not only hidden from the casual eye but also hidden too often from our own selves. We grow so accustomed to being judged on our external structures that we forget to nurture our inner selves, to build on our own foundations. And once we lose faith in our own best instincts, then all we can do is worry about where to put the chairs; we start relying on somebody else's notion of good books. Everything about this insecure calling we call teaching teases and tempts us to tack on one more addition from somebody else's floorplan.

Structures. The word itself has come to be synonymous for me with teacherliness. I'd been teaching what we used to call remedial reading for a couple of years when I stumbled across an Elementary Science Study (ESS) manual called *Structures.* That forty-seven-page guide wiped remedial reading out of my life and changed my very notion of what a teacher is. "Why don't we help these kids find a reason to read?" I asked my boss, who recognized—and supported—a revolution when he saw one. Fortunately, we were moving into a new building, and at the same time I scrapped the contents of the remedial-reading lab, I also wiped out labels and timetables. I announced that henceforth I was a media-resource teacher. I thought I'd invented a new term, one carrying no negative baggage. I wanted people to associate me with the library and in those days we'd never heard of the *resource room.* Because we needed to collect the Title funds New York State provided, I was still a reading teacher on the books but nobody told the kids. Teachers had a list of children who, by law, had to meet with me for the required contact hours per week. But because I opened my door to everybody in the school, no child had a label. All children who could persuade their teachers to let them out of the room were welcome to come to my room for as long as they needed. "Gifted" children showed up right alongside the not-so-gifted, and the students formed remarkable cross-age, mixed-ability partnerships. Because we ignored the bells, children weren't interrupted; they had the time they needed for messing around and making discoveries. Derrick, a boy repeating first grade whose official records labeled him as having "short attention span, difficulty sticking to a task," for example, worked for three hours straight on his proof that fifteen bottle caps on one side of a balance beam weighed the same as fifteen bottle caps on the other side. He set up this proof and then tested it and tested it and tested it. I did not go near him during the entire three hours. His moment of realization was private but profound. Just to make sure, he came back two days later and weighed those bottle caps one more time.

Parents heard so much about the messing around that they asked if they could hold a PTA meeting in my classroom. They didn't want a slide show of our projects; they wanted to come and mess around themselves. And they did.

People cringe when they hear of upwards of thirty children scattered all over a room doing different things. "Where's the structure? The accountability?" are questions I'm often asked. In point of fact, it's much easier to recognize—and account for—what's happening with children involved in twenty-five individual projects than to figure out the significances when twenty-five children work through the same ditto sheet. Or read the same novel.

A crowded room filled with children messing around is in my mind's eye forever. Several children were working on *Structures*. They had contests to see who could build the strongest clay bridge, the highest tower of straws. They watched a film I'd borrowed from the Rensselaer Polytechnic Institute physics department about a bridge collapsing because of wind resonance. They loved that film, watching it over and over. (The PTA also asked to see that film their children talked about nonstop.)

Jeanne, a fifth-grader, was not involved in *Structures*. When she wasn't helping a third-grader construct a dinosaur mobile, she was working on her own *Sound Experiments*. But so much of our learning is sideways. Although students were held responsible for keeping project notebooks, they were free to "waste time," to nose around other kids' projects. Jeanne watched the bridge film half a dozen times and then commented, "Isn't that like the rice experiment?" I still get chills when I recall that moment. Weeks before, Jeanne had taken an oatmeal carton, cut a hole in the side, stretched tissue paper over the top, and put grains of rice on the paper. She noted that when some children shouted into the hole, the rice jumped. Other voices could not make the rice jump. The experiment card directed her to readings that explained how the frequency of some sounds matched the natural frequency at which the air in the box vibrated, causing the rice to jump. Jeanne must have had fifty-three kids shout into her carton before she wrote up the experiment. Weeks later, she was prepared to make the intellectual leap associating the convoluting bridge with the jumping rice. Jeanne needed the shouting and its attendant tomfoolery; she needed the repetition; she needed the freedom and the space to explore, to play, to work — in preparation for that impressive intellectual leap. And what *was* she doing, anyway? Was it science? reading? writing? math? Was it gifted? Remedial? Cooperative? Solitary? Does it matter?

People traveled from other cities to see that classroom; the state education department gave me a couple of awards; the library school gave me money; an official at the U.S. Department of the Interior phoned one day to tell me I was terrific. But educational hoopla has a shelf life shorter than that of cream puffs, and one year's innovation is next year's limp noodle. Two years after I created that classroom, a newly hired deputy chief administrator who needed to establish her own priorities assigned me to supervise criterion-referenced tests throughout the district.

I lasted three weeks as a pencil pusher, and then I went to the superintendent and insisted on a transfer. I did not quite quote e. e. cummings' "There is some shit I will not eat" — but I came close. I told the superintendent I would take any *teaching* job in the district, but I had to teach. And thus it was that I came to set up a storefront classroom for forty extremely disaffected high school students who had been excluded from the regular campus.

A lot of people thought that assignment was my punishment for rocking the boat. The people who thought it most of all were my students: they were convinced that something must be wrong with any teacher who had to work with *them*. How wrong they were. We were given an empty building, and we created a school. Not only did we choose the chairs, but choice of the curriculum — from reading, writing, science, and social studies to risk-taking and responsibility — was ours too. After the students and I bought the overstuffed red velvet sofa, I ordered lots of periodicals, lots of paperbacks, and lots of ESS supplies. Students accompanied me on visits to used-book stores. They enjoyed giving me a hard time because I wouldn't order *The National Enquirer*. Anyone who teaches reluctant readers of any age knows that their most frustrating quality is their ennui. Those kids firmly believed there is nothing (legal) under the sun that will spark their attention, never mind their enthusiasm. I had faith that the daily paper, some blockbuster books, and the investigation of the structural capabilities of an index card could surprise, amaze, and maybe even delight and challenge my students.

I'll never forget the excitement and wonder on the faces of those tuned-out teenagers when Mike's toothpick bridge held forty-five pounds of books before it began to sag and creak. Staring at his bridge, Mike said, "I didn't know I had the patience to do anything like this."

Even an architectural graduate student at Rensselaer Polytechnic Institute was impressed. I invited her in as a "structures consultant" and she told us that not even RPI requires barebones toothpick bridges; they use pea connectors. "Oh god," moaned Mike, "You mean there was an easier way?" And he puffed up more than ever—knowing that not only had he succeeded, but he'd done it the pure way, the tough way. And he'd done it all by himself.

How many times in our curricular planning do we allow the time and space for a seven-year-old and a fifteen-year-old to discover that they have patience? That they can achieve without shortcuts or props? Without remediation? There is no question but Mike was Derrick's older soul brother. Mike echoed his fellow teenagers when he said, "The one thing I hated about the regular school was every time you started something, the bell would ring and you'd have to go start something else." The structure of regular school seldom gives you three hours to weigh bottle caps or three weeks to build a bridge.

Don't look to the ESS *Structures* manual if you want a recipe for making toothpick bridges. Toothpick bridges aren't even suggested in the manual. But other bridge projects are, and, as with all undertakings worth their salt, one thing leads to another. Students who think they don't like to read, be they nine years old or fifteen, find informational books irresistible. We had books about killer bees and motorcycles; we had books about bridges. While he was reading about bridges, Mike noticed an article in the newspaper about a man who built a toothpick model of the Eifel Tower and wondered if he couldn't build a toothpick bridge. The marvel of the ESS manuals is that they are not *how-to* documents; instead, they nudge and prod and provoke teachers and students to think for themselves, to extend themselves.

Yes, there was a bit of luck that Mike saw the newspaper article. But serendipity comes to people who can recognize sparks of illumination. If I have had any core reading list through the years, then newspapers are it. If your goal is to help students become lifetime readers, then newspapers are a great place to start; hook a fourteen-year-old on newspapers and you've hooked him for life. I required seventh-graders to start the period by reading newspapers for ten minutes. Convincing the administration that I didn't want newspaper kits, not watered down student newspapers, but fifteen subscriptions to the local paper, plus one copy each of *The New York Times*, *New York Post*, and *The*

Daily News was not easy. I required my high schoolers to read the newspaper fifteen minutes a day—in addition to their half hour of extended reading. I carry in my mind's eye a host of beautiful serendipities that this newspaper habit provoked over the years.

And the routines of basic experimentation as well as the bursts of discovery in *Structures* showed me that teaching first-graders and sixth-graders and high school and college students is much more the same than it is different. Roland S. Barth revealed the basic premise under it all. When he was still a principal he described his first visit to Elementary Science Study. He asked a lot of questions and seemed to get few answers:

> "Can I see the lesson plans for a unit?"
> —We have none.
> "How does a teacher teach without plans?"
> You put the materials out and see what children do with them. When children ask a question or need something, you help them. (Barth, 1972, p. xvii)

It's easy to see why such a philosophy would drive most administrators nuts. Most teachers too. What's hard for teachers is not passing out paper or maintaining time-on-task or choosing good books. The hardest thing for a teacher is to keep her hands off. And her mouth shut.

Structures is no longer available from Education Development Center, the folks who received National Science Foundation funds to develop the ESS manuals; they're scrambling for a $24 million payoff for subverting their good idea. When I read recently that the National Science Foundation had granted Educational Development Center (EDC) nearly $24 million to come up with a new hands-on elementary science curriculum, I phoned EDC and asked what was wrong with the old hands-on ideas they had developed more than two decades ago. They didn't like the question. After all, if you can get mega-bucks to improve an old idea, then that idea *must* need improving; that's the American way. After being transferred, put on hold, and disconnected, I still wouldn't let go of the question and finally reached a cheerful woman who explained the need to make things neater, more straight-forward, the need to give teachers frameworks and strategies so they can present lessons to their students and their students can produce outcomes. In short, they're designing things so teachers know ahead of time what they will teach and students know what they're expected to learn. When my informant found out I hold in sacred trust half a dozen of the original EDC Elementary Science Study teachers' guides, she admitted, without flourish, "You old diehards are not going to like the revision." (The original *Structures* manual is still available: Delta Education, Box M, Nashua, NH 03061. While you're at it, you may want to ask about the other thirty-five ESS manuals they sell.)

Donald Graves worries about why bad things happen to good ideas. Graves suggests that the reason science and social-studies processes died on the vine was that the teacher was reduced to a spectator role. When somebody hands you your structure—tells you what you should teach and what the kids should learn—then you are a spectator. Graves expresses concern that writing and reading processes may fare no better if teachers allow themselves to become spectators. Graves is the first to lament that when teachers worry whether they should do the five-step Graves or the seven-step Graves, they have misunderstood the point. They are spectators, not teachers.

In my darker moments I wonder if any idea can succeed if it can't be linked to textbooks and worksheets. Certainly few people are anxious to make "restructure" synonymous with "simplify" or "inexpensive." There's something about an educationist that loves a system, a 46-step plan, a checklist, a core reading list. And teachers who try to subvert neat and tidy structures never have an easy time. When I taught third grade, my district decided to invite teachers into the book-selection process, and I served on the language arts textbook selection committee. At our first meeting we discovered that middle- and upper-grade teachers wanted a bigger and better grammar book, one with lots of drills. Third-grade teachers seemed more open to the idea of abandoning student textbooks in favor of a teacher-resource pack of half a dozen professional books about language acquisition and development. And so we third-grade teachers split off from the pack and formed our own subcommittee.

Certain high administrators must have heard what was afoot because three of them showed up at our next meeting, one that brought together all the third-grade teachers in the district. The deputy chief administrator, the very same one who selected me to administer criterion-referenced tests, insisted we needed not just a grammar text but a spelling text too. In a tone implying that only good spellers will pass through the Pearly Gates, she announced, "A child doesn't need to be able to read a word to learn how to spell it correctly." If there were such a thing as a text devoted to commas, I'm sure she would have insisted we buy that, too.

With this kind of pressure from the top, you might think there was no hope. But teachers have a way of surprising you, especially when the vote is by secret ballot. When the vote was taken, the majority favored the teacher-resource packs over individual student texts. Months went by. Some of us sent suggestions for teacher-resource books to the deputy chief administrator's deputy. Finally, the third-grade teachers were called together again—to vote on the textbook issue. When we muttered, "We thought we already voted," we were told that vote was "unofficial." This time we voted by a show of hands and the outcome was closer, but the "no text" people won again. The next day the deputy chief administrator's deputy issued a memo calling for a signed ballot from every third-grade teacher. She said this was "in fairness to the teachers who were absent from the meeting." Results of that tally were never announced but the third-grade teachers were called to meet one more time. At last, I caught on: we were going to vote until we got it right. The deputy chief administrator's deputy made an impassioned plea that we be sensitive to "our image of excellence as perceived by the public." She asked us, "How can the public have faith in our commitment to excellence if we don't even have a language arts textbook?" Whereupon third-grade teachers voted to provide every student in the district with a language arts textbook. My only satisfaction was that even in the face of all that pressure, the vote was close.

Months later, my third-graders asked if we were ever going to use those new books stacked on the window ledge. I told them they could use them whenever they wanted. And they did. Every time we had *choices*, five or six children would choose to "play school." Someone would be teacher and pass out either the language arts texts or the basal workbooks. (Although I did not use a basal, in the name of excellence and standards a classroom set of workbooks was delivered to my classroom.) The teacher would wave the pointer and yell at the students to "do their pages." They loved using the teachers' manuals to correct those pages. Sometimes I wonder if it's like my friend who carefully excludes sugar from her children's diet. Every chance those kids get, they binge on junk food. Given the chance, my students binged on the forbidden workbooks.

That experience has made me quite sympathetic with the folks in California who have come up with a literature plan. Bad things happen to good people. Bad things happen to good literature too. Last year I was invited out to California to take a look at the California Literature Project. Good things are happening: teachers are excited about literature. They are themselves reading and talking. But bad things are happening too. In developing lists of books to fulfill the official plan of "a systematic, well-organized core program in which the overlap of selections at more than one grade span level is avoided," there is a whole lot of argument among teachers over who "gets" particular books. Second- and third-grade teachers, for example, come close to shedding blood over who "gets" *Charlotte's Web*. And ninth-graders get *Great Expectations*. Honest. I met a lot of teachers in California who, in the name of a new, innovative structure, have decreed that *Great Expectations* is the book that every ninth-grader in the district must read: gifted students and not-so-gifted students all read this book so that they have a common piece of literature they can discuss. If this doesn't make you weep, what will?

I wonder why otherwise reasonable people go sort of crazy when book-choosing time rolls around. For one thing, terminal hypocrisy sets in. The same people who swap copies of Judith Krantz and Stephen King and Irving Wallace in the faculty room put Dickens on their core lists. Core lists, it seems, are made by people who feel confident in their knowledge of what *other people* should read. In 1969 I made a case that the execrable reading taste revealed in bestseller lists is a direct result of the artificiality, sentimentality, and just plain bad writing of basal readers ("To Hell with Rip Van Winkle," *Intersections*, Center for Urban and Environmental Studies, Troy, NY, 1969). Why would we expect things to have changed in just two decades when, as Larry Cuban reminds us, for all the periodic hustle and bustle, the pedagogy in schools hasn't changed much in the past one hundred years?

I've never met a required book list I liked. Such lists are always prescriptive and retrospective. They keep us looking over our shoulders, maintaining a static rather than a dynamic notion of culture. And the worst part is that once you let a core list into your life, it's very hard to dislodge it. Asking a faculty to change a recommended book list and getting a new list approved by administrators and the board of education is like asking someone to move a graveyard. If you're persistent, stubborn, and intractable, you may get a few new items added; you'll never get old bones removed.

Who's afraid of Charles Dickens? I am! Putting Dickens on a required core list, insisting that every eighth-grader must read *A Christmas Carol* and every ninth-grader must read *Great Expectations*, victimizes children. I have nothing against Dickens as literature of choice. If individual teachers know and love Dickens and know and love their students — and feel they can make a match — then God bless those teachers, every one of them. But California teachers I talked with lamented that Dickens is not a personal choice; traveling under the name of standards and excellence, it is simply what is required. Others defended the choice on the grounds that it is meritorious for every child to have a classic in common, that not-so-able children are invited into a community of learners and share this experience with all their classmates. I see it as a heartbreaking requirement. Forcefeeding Dickens will exclude many students from knowing the personal joy that literature can bring, a joy that is their right. I worry not just that those vulnerable students will never try Dickens again; I worry they will be scared off from dipping into any literature again. Remember that bromide from some years back, "This is the first day of the rest of your life"? We need to choose our books as though today is the last day of our lives — and theirs — to turn kids onto reading.

Poet-farmer-teacher Wendell Berry gives us a wonderful image of what happens when people insist on unanimity over diversity. He gives us "crazy old Mrs. Gaines who sang of One Lord, one Faith, and one Cornbread" (p. 26). Wendell Berry never even hints that crazy old Mrs. Gaines might have been a high school English teacher, but certainly the irony of high school is that students' literary choices become ever more restricted. I can sympathize with teachers who regard it as an excess of diversity to say to their students, "Choose your own books," but surely when the core book is *Great Expectations* we must recognize that such lists are taking us too far in the direction of received dogma. And as Wendell Berry points out, they had to lock crazy old Mrs. Gaines up in a room because "For her, to be free was only to be lost."

I used to ask teachers, "What would happen if you were shut up in a room with thirty of your colleagues and not allowed to leave until you'd all read the same book?" But that's exactly what happened in California. The California Literature Project brought teachers together during the summer and subjected them to an intensive, rigorous study of James Joyce's *Ulysses*. The next summer another group studied Proust. When I met those teachers at a weekend reunion, I heard lots of groans and laughter, lots of talk about "surviving" Joyce and "surviving" Proust. I both admire and am appalled by the notion. I can acknowledge and even applaud the power of their intellectual endeavor. I witnessed firsthand the sense of community and joint accomplishment it engendered. But I wonder if *survival* — getting through a book — is the literary model we want for our classrooms. I wonder how many of those teachers have, on their own, read more Joyce, more Proust? How many of them have read more Irish writers, more French writers?

As an English major I avoided courses on eighteenth-century literature because I'd discovered on my own that *Tom Jones* was just about the greatest book ever written, and I was afraid some professorial pedant would ruin it for me. Even though I was led through *Moby Dick* by one of the best professors I ever had, and even though *Moby Dick* was his passion (how many teachers build an altar — complete with lighted candles — in the front of the room with *the book* in the place of reverence?), I felt only relief when we finally got through it. My only real emotion for the book was, "I made it; thank God it's over." I never looked at Melville again — until about five years ago when, piqued by a scholarly comment, I decided to take another look. I'm not at all surprised that my eighteen-year-old self couldn't appreciate Melville's grand passion, couldn't see his humor. My recent pleasure in the book convinces me I just might even be ready for George Eliot. A few years ago I asked some people I respect a lot what books they would commend to teachers. Katherine Paterson and Robert Coles both spoke so eloquently of the richness of *Middlemarch* that I know one day I'll have to relinquish my school-forced detestation and give it a try.

I don't want my students to survive literature. I want my students to read out of curiosity, out of a need to be informed, out of an anticipation of fun. I want my students to read widely — and fairly casually. Time enough for them to plumb the depths of literary analysis — if they want to do that sort of thing — when they get to college. Since my first year of teaching when *Silas Marner*, *Julius Caesar*, and *Johnny Tremain* were on my school's required list, I've never been able to bring myself to tell a student he *had* to read any particular book. Students are so diverse. And as publishing imprints abound, we have available a bountiful supply of limitless possibility, books as diverse as the children in our care. What is the need for "one cornbread"?

For me, coaxing students into reading is rather like growing African violets. Twenty years ago my husband and I ordered some seeds. The seeds were so infinitesimal we thought the packet was empty. And by the time the seeds finally germinated months later, we had almost given up hope. I forget the exact timeline but we didn't have flowers for several years. And young readers are a whole lot like African violet seeds. They need a good environment; they need to be given space and time to develop. They need, in Jane Hansen's (1987) words, to be led "from behind," their language learning capabilities supported indirectly through the environment we offer them. We can't force readers; we must nurture them. My violets are still in brilliant bloom. And Denise is blooming too. Denise is proof that classroom habits can last a lifetime. One of my articles of faith has been to exchange notes with my students every day. Even at her angriest, Denise, the student so recalcitrant she had the distinction of failing seventh grade twice, always wrote, and she still writes today. Denise writes of taking her kids to the library every week. She says her kids like *Flat Stanley* almost as much as I do. Denise writes about introducing her children to the Stupids, Frog and Toad, and Madeline, as well as Stanley. Denise writes, "I can't wait until they're old enough for Gilly Hopkins. I want to read that book again." I like to think Denise learned something important in my class — and it has nothing to do with whether or not she ever read someone else's notion of a classic. I measure my success not in how many children I can push through *Great Expectations*, but in the Denises who are tempted to read a book twenty years after they leave my care.

There's another *structures* kind of moral to this story. I was so convinced that our classroom letter exchange was the best pedagogical tool I'd ever used that in 1978 I sent an article about it to a professional journal. When it was rejected, I sent the article to another professional journal and another. Not even half a dozen form-letter regrets could deter me from a good idea. My students let me know every day that the experts were wrong. Letter writing might lack pedagogical pizazz but my students let me know it was crucial in our lives. Of course, my error was not in the process but in the nomenclature. There is something about our profession that loves a two-dollar word. Nonetheless, to this day I can't stomach calling letters between a teacher and her students *interactive journals*.

Too much of what travels under the banners of official excellence bespeaks a contempt for students and for teachers too. Core lists show a lack of trust in teachers, in students, and in literature. Core lists have a way of turning into literature laws, hemming teachers in and fencing kids out. Core lists have a way of telling students that the only good authors are the dead ones. Literature that becomes itemized, formalized, and, most dangerously, standardized dies. What we have left is a graveyard of books. What we need is a dynamic model of literature, one that encourages our students to become lifelong readers, one that encourages them to become parents who read to their children. This won't happen if *student choice* is not central to the program.

I stressed this idea of student choice in a talk to the California Literature Project and a number of Project members wrote me notes accusing me of anarchism. Student choice, they insisted, is fine and dandy for recreational reading, but for *literature study* the teacher must choose. Left on their own, teachers insisted, students won't move beyond *Sweet Valley High* books.

I know for a fact that this is not true. It's not true with first-graders; it's not true with high schoolers. When you surround children with the sounds and sense of wonderful language, they respond. They make good choices. When my third-graders and I won one hundred free books in a paperback book contest, I told them they could each choose a book to keep and then choose four each for our classroom library. No blue-ribbon book-selection committee could have taken their charge more seriously, and the list the children came up with was impressive. No one wasted a choice. They chose fiction such as *The Little House* books, *Owls in the Family*, *Frog and Toad*, *Ralph S. Mouse*; they chose mysteries, poetry, nonfiction; they chose hard books and easy books. "But not too easy," they reminded one another. Over and over I heard a book dismissed with the comment, "You'd only want to read that one once."

The same thing happened with seventh- and eighth-graders. When I was still a remedial reading teacher with an inherited lab filled with ugly little controlled-vocabulary paragraphs, I decided the best way to revitalize the program was to give each of my students a book coupon redeemable for a paperback once a month in a local bookstore. I took my students for their first visit. They quickly passed over *Snoopy* books, hairstyling books, and series romances. Amazing to me, 90 percent of those inner-city remedial students chose such classics as Shakespeare, Twain, and Hawthorne—yes, and Dickens too—for their first book. They'd pick up Shakespeare and say, "Oh yeah, I've heard of that." They seemed to like the idea of owning an important book even though they had no intention of reading it. After that, students visited the store on their own. They brought back sports biographies, young adult novels, mysteries, fairy tales, and adult bestsellers. Two sisters pooled their coupons and saved up until they had enough for a hardback cookbook. Sylvia complained that every time she chose her book she had a fight with her mother over who got to read it first. I told Sylvia she must be making good choices. One day Sylvia's mother visited my classroom, wanting to see if I had any more good books she might borrow.

Isn't that what education is all about? Helping people to make their own choices? Helping them establish some sort of criteria for making good choices? Who's going to provide the core books for our students when they're on their own? I hear a lot of talk in California about giving teachers *a sense of ownership*. There's no mention of the students' ownership and I'd certainly put money on my supposition that no student was included on the vote for *Great Expectations*. Anyway, I have grave doubts about this thing called *a sense of ownership*. Either it's yours or it ain't, and twenty years messing around in schools has shown me that if you want it, you gotta grab it. Anybody starts talking about a sense of ownership in my house and I'm going to count the silverware.

In our restructuring for real literature, aren't we taking things just a bit too seriously? Over and over I see that word *worthy* in connection with literature in the classroom. My third-graders learned a whole lot about how language works from riddle books, Amelia Bedelia, and Morris and Borris. When short-story writer *par excellence* Tobias Wolff was in high school, his older brother Geoffrey wrote him a letter from Princeton, advising him on the great core books he should read if he ever hoped to amount to anything. The rather pretentious and pedantic Geoffrey was ahead of his time with his core list for his brother's enlightenment. Not long ago, Tobias sent his brother a copy of that long-ago letter with a note, "OK, Mr. Smarty Pants, I'm a professor and I still haven't read this stuff."

The real issue is not whether the literature we bring to our students is worthy; the real issue is whether we are willing to take risks in the classroom. Edward Abbey was a wonderful gadfly and, for me, a mentor. When he died recently, I knew I'd lost a friend. He wrote often of the need for self-testing. He warns us not to become settled in our ways, "content as pigs in a warm manure pile." Abbey (1977) wrote that to be alive is to take risks. To be always safe and secure is death. In Abbey's words:

> The permissive society? What else? I love America because it *is* a confused, chaotic mess, and I hope we can keep it this way for at least another thousand years. The permissive society is the free society, the open society. Who gave us permission to live this way? Nobody did. *We* did. And that's the way it should be—only more so. The best cure for the ills of democracy is democracy. (p. 230)

It comes as no surprise that Abbey liked to quote Walt Whitman. "Resist much," advises Whitman in his (1959) preface to *Leaves of Grass*: "Love the earth and the sun and the animals. Despise riches. Give alms to everyone that asks. Stand up for the stupid and crazy. . . . Take off your hat to nothing known or unknown. . . . Re-examine all you have been told at school or church or in any book and dismiss whatever insults your own soul." Who would dare to put this on a core list? And yet the best cure for the ills of education is to risk much, to resist much. The best cure for the ills of education is more diversity, not less.

In a deep sense students are more the same than they are different, but on the surface there is a whole lot of diversity. How can we choose our curricula ahead of time? How can the same books be altogether "right" year after year after year? One group of third-graders loved *Amelia Bedelia*, but next year's crew, a more sophisticated bunch, thought that was "baby stuff." *Trumpet of the Swan* is on California's fourth-grade list. I would have fought to my last gasp anyone who tried to prevent me from reading it with one of my third grades. Much as we all loved it, I read the book with children only that one time. New years bring new needs, new books. How about *Sarah, Plain and Tall*? Who *gets* it? Do the rest of us just have to sit there smoldering with envy?

In his poem "Traveling at Home," from his book by the same name, Wendell Berry (1989) reminds us

> Even in a country you know by heart
> it's hard to go the same way twice.
> The life of the going changes.
> The chances change and make a new way.
> Any tree or stone or bird
> can be the bud of a new direction. The
> natural correction is to make intent
> of accident. To get back before dark
> is the art of going.

A teacher whom I've never met but with whom I've developed a friendship through correspondence put it this way: "I've taught first grade for twenty-three years and I've never done it the same way twice." I mentioned this to a longtime colleague who has taught fourth and fifth grades for more than twenty years and she agreed. "The year I get things right, the year I'm satisfied, I'll know it's time to quit."

Borrowing from Judith Viorst, I offer my version of "If I Were in Charge of the World":

> If I were in charge of the world
> I'd cancel facilitators,
> Friday spellings,
> Pizza bribes, and also
> Questions at the end of the story.

If I were in charge of the world
You could read *Charlotte's Web*
In any grade you wanted.
You could even read it twice.
If I were in charge of the world
There'd be a million million
Pages of delight,
Instead of thirty-two copies
Of three novels
Somebody else chose.
If I were in charge of the world
Nobody under age 40 would be encouraged to read *Moby Dick*,
No books would come by decree.
And a person who said knock-knock riddle books with pop-up
    pages are a quintessential part of a reading program
Would still be allowed to be
In charge of the world.

REFERENCES

Abbey, E. (1977). *The journey home*. New York: E. P. Dutton.

Barth, R. S. (1972). *Open education and the American school*. New York: Agathon Press, Inc.

Berry, W. (1989). Meditation in the spring rain. In *Traveling at home* (pp. 26−28). San Francisco: North Point Press.

———. (1989). Traveling at home. In *Traveling at home* (p. 23). San Francisco: North Point Press.

Blake, W. (1982). "The Marriage of Heaven and Hell." In David E. Erdman, ed., *The Complete Poetry and Prose of William Blake* (p. 35). Berkeley: Univ. of California Press.

Cummings, E. E. "I Sing of Olaf." In Oscar Williams, ed., (1955). *The New Pocket Anthology of American Verse*, New York: Washina Square Press.

Hansen, J. (1987). *When writers read*. Portsmouth, NH: Heinemann.

Ohanian, S. (1969). To hell with Rip Van Winkle. *Intersections*. Troy, NY: Center for Urban and Environmental Studies.

Viorst, J. (1984). *If I Were in Charge of the World and Other Worries*. New York: Atheneum.

Whitman, W. (1959). Preface To 1855 Edition of "Leaves of Grass." In James E. Miller Jr, ed, *Complete Poetry and Selected Prose of Walt Whitman* (pp. 412−427). Boston: Houghton Mifflin.

Finding the Structures Within

Martha West
Gwinnett Open Campus High School
Norcross, Georgia

*I*n a curious juxtaposition of experiences, I have spent much of the past year participating in our school system's strategic planning process, where the word *restructuring* was dropped into every conversation at least a half dozen times. Then, when I awarded myself a long weekend at the beach to recuperate from strategic planning and the NCTE convention, I took along a book called *Free Play: Improvisation in Life and Art*, by Stephen Nachmanovitch (1990). Perhaps I should have read it sooner. Nachmanovitch is a musician, among other things. He writes about music, painting, teaching, learning, and life—very Zen. He has forced me back into the graduate-student mode: I dug out a highlighter pen and started keeping a response journal. I've been talking back to him so much that I was disappointed to finish the book.

This chapter is mostly a conversation with Nachmanovitch, or perhaps it is an improvisation on his theme. We shall see.

Improvisation, as Nachmanovitch defines it, is nothing at all like impromptu or whim or impulse. It is composition, in a specific context, through internalized techniques and knowledge, influenced by the dynamics of participants, instruments, audience, and skill, and limited by rules. Improvisation takes place "in real time" (p. 18). For musicians,

> The time of inspiration, the time of technically structuring and realizing the music, the time of playing it, and the time of communicating with the audience, as well as ordinary clock time, are all one. (p. 18)

For teachers,

> In a real classroom, . . . there are live people with personal needs and knowledge. . . . Planning an agenda of learning without knowing who is going to be there, what their strengths and weaknesses are, . . . prevents surprises and prevents learning. . . . The teacher's art is to connect, in real time, the living bodies of the students with the living body of the knowledge. (p. 20)

Neither is improvisation something that just happens without preparation or practice: "We still engage in the important practice of planning and scheduling—not to rigidly lock in the future but to tune up the self" (p. 21). Learning, like living, involves making up what we do as we go along, using the materials of skill and experience that we have acquired up to that point in our lives.

Improvisation and Restructuring

The distinction between what Nachmanovitch calls "scripted behavior" (p. 20) and improvisation is of special importance to teachers as we talk about restructuring our schools and our classrooms. As teachers we know that we do not structure learning. The metaphors that we choose to describe learning—networks, scaffoldings, webs—imply that learning happens in and among learners. We structure environments, external contexts that facilitate, accommodate, and complement the structures within the learners. That is, we take what we know about how learning works and we eliminate obstructions. At best, we influence learning.

We also know that the structures of learning are both idiosyncratic and universal. We recognize patterns and processes that we all share. Schools as we know them couldn't exist without this commonality. Nor, for that matter, could communities.

But learning is also idiosyncratic because, for one thing, learning is driven by the need to learn. We learn to operate a telephone in order to communicate with people out of earshot. We learn about the stock market in order to secure our retirement income (and some of us, having learned, choose other forms of investment). We learn to dress appropriately for our jobs, but we don't all dress for the same job.

In school children learn to listen for certain signals from their teachers. At the same time, they are learning to listen to different kinds of signals from their friends, families, and employers. The structure of learning, the symbol system, is the same, but the needs, the applications, and the desired outcomes are different. What children learn is how to improvise.

As teachers, we learn techniques that enable us to be successful, yet no one technique guarantees success in every situation. We would no more use the same lesson plan every day than we would go into class each day with no plan at all. Success depends on repertoire and on our sensitivity to the needs of the moment. We know that we must attend to the social structures within our classrooms. Often our most important decisions concern conflict, boredom, failure, or success — our own as well as our students'.

In fact, it is difficult to use the word *structure* to refer to something as kaleidoscopic and ephemeral as learning. Talk about restructuring makes me worry that we are talking about building a different-shaped box to put teachers and students in, to put learning in. There is a danger that even the most enlightened and right-headed structures will still be, because they are elements of an institution, cages.

More than any other discipline, ours has everything to gain from restructuring. The move toward integration, toward cooperative learning, and toward local school autonomy all imply attention to communication "skills": active listening, articulate speech, writing, and reading to construct meaning individually and socially in every corner of the school. As long as traditional institutional structures are in place, teachers in the vast majority of high schools have little hope of reducing class size, of constructing larger blocks of class time for writing and reading workshops, of gaining adequate access to computer labs. We must approach this latest of reform movements with prepared imaginations, with confidence, and with flexibility. We must assure ourselves of a voice in the changes that will affect us.

There is a real risk, however, that we ourselves will be unable to envision the possibilities, that our own imaginations will be inadequate to the task. We have to trust our own expertise, which tells us that teaching and learning are improvisatory acts. The structures that count are those we create and revise daily in our classrooms.

Elements of Improvisation

Practice as performance: A commitment to process

Practice is what we do every day. Perhaps physicians have an advantage over the rest of us in that they "practice" medicine — a different meaning from "practice" teaching! Nachmanovitch describes practice as an activity that has intrinsic value. Our "Western idea of practice is to acquire a skill. It is very much related to our work ethic, which enjoins us to endure struggle or boredom now in return for future rewards" (p. 67). No wonder so many of us gave up the piano or the violin. No wonder so many of our students give up on usage or vocabulary. In order to make the most of learning, we need to find value in the process itself.

We have learned to look at the writing process this way, and we have begun to look at learning this way. We worship at the altar of Process. But our schools are structured for outcomes, for product. So we find ourselves trying to balance between the two, to keep in mind the end product even as we pour our energy and attention into the process, the music-making in our classrooms.

The concept of improvisation can help us reduce this tension. Nothing that I have read or heard so eloquently describes the way teaching feels as Nachmanovitch's description of music-making:

> In the act of improvising we can do a number of things consciously. We can say to ourselves, This theme needs repeating; This new part of the material needs to be sewn together with the part that came a few minutes ago; This is horrible—cut it short or change it; This is great—let it grow; This feels like I'm approaching the end; and so forth. We're operating on a continuous stream of emerging pattern. (p. 32)

We work with the objectives, with the curriculum, but we work in the moment. I know what I'm supposed to teach, that is, what students are supposed to be able to perform when I've finished with them. But the most important learning, often, is in the music we make. Hearing ourselves make it, discovering what we can do, then stretching— challenging ourselves and one another to make it more complex, more elaborate—or simpler, finding the simple theme at the center. Students *will* be able to recognize theme in a novel, to analyze character in a short story. I trust that they will, so I can improvise with them. We will have outcomes when we need them. Mayher, in *Uncommon Sense* (1990), says, "*Genuine learning should be personally rewarding both for the sense of confidence which comes from building competence and from the inherent fascination of the things themselves*" (p. 96, author's italics).

It is a paradox, trusting that the learning will occur if we concentrate on the activity for its own sake. I think this is possible to a great extent because of the nature of language teaching and learning. Much of what we teach is what people do—talk, listen, read, write, think. Our practice is performance.

In fact, we have always lived with this paradox. How often we comment to each other, usually when a former student comes back to visit, that we never know what students have learned from us, seldom hear how we have influenced a life. If we could be certain of nothing but the scores on exit exams, then we would have little to show for our lives' work. Fortunately, we are sure of more. We know the "teachable moment," and we know when the music is flowing. Our students know it, too, and any reasonable visitor to our classrooms knows it. What's more, if asked to do so, we can reflect on the music and can report what happened. This isn't random and it isn't coincidental. It is the solid improvisational performance of a group of confident learners working together.

Faith in process also implies faith in playfulness. "Anytime we perform an activity for an outcome," Nachmanovitch says, "even if it's a high, noble, or admirable end, we are not totally *in* that activity. That is the lesson we draw from watching a child disappear in play" (p. 146). And play, in this sense of unself-conscious concentration and experimentation for its own sake, is a powerful tool of learning. It involves suspending judgment; it means being open to unpredictable possibilities; it means forgetting to watch the clock. When creative play is at work in my classroom, I greet it with a kind of reverence, a certain degree of awe.

A broad repertoire of techniques and resources

Nachmanovitch says that improvisation depends on "having technique to burn — having more powerful and flexible means available to us than we need in any given situation" (p. 44). This is the heart of my response and my belief in improvisational teaching. Doing the same thing over and over again, pulling out last year's plans and recycling them for this year's students, is a mind-deadening, self-destructive act. Through practice (daily, in process), reflection, and professional inter-action, most of us have "technique to burn."

Improvisational teaching means putting together our prior knowledge and experience with the daily revisions of our work. What happens when a lesson doesn't work? We say, "Why didn't it work? It went great with the last class." Something in the class? Something in me? Or something in the organism that is the-class-and-me?

We know what to do, and we know it intuitively. Intuition isn't magic. Nachmanovitch's definition resonates with others that I have come to accept: "Intuition is a synaptic summation, our whole nervous system balancing and combining multivariate complexities in a single flash" (pp. 39–40). We grasp the thing all at once without going through all the steps. Of course, we are trained to go through all the steps. We need to be. But, have you ever been on Step Two of a six-step lesson when the students are already on Step Six? Tune your instrument. Watch for it. What happens then?

Teachers need to trust their internalized expertise. We guide learning by a series of on-the-spot adjustments, more or less intuitive decisions about what to do next and where to go next. Carrying multiple copies of a half dozen poems to class is one of the ways that I prepare myself to improvise. One group may settle into a discussion of theme, in which case I need another poet's view for comparison. Another may need help with recognizing irony, so a different poet's voice provides additional practice. Frequently, five or six groups of students head to different corners of the room with different poems, their work defined by the dynamics of the moment, the outcomes of their work depending on the dynamics of their interactions.

Does this mean I don't plan? A weekly lesson plan (or a unit outline or whatever form a long-range plan takes) is useful. But it limits us by making us feel guilty if we don't stick to it. Planning, at its best, involves purposeful reflection, thinking about outcomes, tuning our minds to the possible ways to achieve those outcomes, remembering past experiences, and setting up contexts for improvisation.

Reflection also makes me think of revision. How does a teacher go from improvisation to revision? Reflection, I think. In class one day, an impulse. It works, but when I try to re-create it next period, it flops. Why? The event grew out of the context. Trying to re-create the event exactly in a different context doesn't work. Still, the event has value for teaching. It may be better to go back to the original plan second period; meanwhile, jot down what happened and how it happened, seek the *core* of the experience.

Once, a few years ago, I decided to use paintings to help students explore their thinking and responses to poetry. I showed slides of several paintings, all twentieth century and nonrealistic. Students wrote down and shared their initial responses, and we constructed interpretations from their comments. Then we used the same process to get past our automatic paralysis in the face of modern poetry. The first time I tried it, it worked so well that I immediately turned it into a proposal for a talk at a teachers' conference. Fortunately for me, even before the conference, I tried it again, and it didn't work. Different students didn't like the group of slides that had ignited the imaginations of my first class. They wouldn't go past "What a weird painting! That makes no sense to me!" They taught me to add some Impressionists to the mix, and Andrew Wyeth. The paintings activity seldom works exactly as it did the first time, but it has developed some interesting variations. Sometimes we use paintings *and* music.

Ruthless editing is part of the technique. If something doesn't work, we reflect and revise. Nothing ever works exactly the same way twice. The best strategies are the open-ended ones, the ones that can work a number of ways. Says Nachmanovitch, "Mastery means responsibility, ability to respond in real time to the need of the moment" (p. 41). Like a vacation trip, learning is often most rewarding when our carefully mapped plans are forced to detour onto unexpected paths.

A true partnership of learners

This includes the one referred to as "teacher." Teachers, like musicians, improvise alone, the solo turn, and *ensemble*, as members of a group that includes their students. Group improvisation assumes a coming together, a harmonizing of different artists and instruments, each artist a configuration of skills and experiences. How does the group make music — or learning? Not, according to Nachmanovitch, by all doing the same thing at the same time. Nachmanovitch makes a distinction between education and training. "Education," he says, "must tap into the close relationship between play and exploration; there must be permission to explore and express" (p. 118). Training, on the other hand, has as its purpose "monoculture," a world in which everyone does everything in exactly the same way. Ensemble work fails if everyone plays the same instrument in the same way. It fails if one person determines the outcome. Unison may be smooth, but it's boring. The texture of music is in the tension of differences — dissonances resolved, solo turns, harmonies elaborated.

Nachmanovitch also speaks of *entrainment*, "the silent rhythm of working together" (p. 99). This is that phenomenon by which two people, walking along the street together, find themselves in step. Music, with its steady rhythms and tempi, has great power to draw us along. So, however, has the work of an ensemble of learners. I have seen students write poems in a room full of their peers, poems that amazed the poets; and the only explanation that I can manage is that the talk and "word shaking" and reading aloud, followed by silence and concentration in one another's company, produce powerful results among those who "never" write poems, as well as those who "must" be alone to write.

How can we create an ensemble where everyone doesn't learn the same thing in the same way at the same time, but without descending into chaos? Improvisation isn't the same thing as cooperative learning. It isn't a method. A true improvisatory ensemble may integrate any number of instructional patterns. It certainly includes passages performed solo by the teacher, or by a single student. I think it must be characterized by listening more than any other action, listening as a musician listens *while he plays* for what the others are doing, for where the piece is going, for what comes next.

Musicians tune their instruments to one another's instruments. They listen skillfully. How do we tune our instruments in the classroom? In a class where students and teachers are engaged in listening and responding to one another, are reading and writing and thinking, their instruments begin to be in tune. "What we discover, mysteriously, is that in tuning the instrument we tune the spirit" (p. 55).

Tune your instrument to mine, or I will tune mine to yours. Or I will play my solo and you will know when it's over, when it's time to join in—because you are listening so well, to me and to the music we are making together.

Remember this scenario? The teacher is lecturing, talking away, as she is (I am) wont to do. A student jumps in, making a connection. What happens next? Is this a solo performance or an ensemble improvisation? What the teacher does next determines the quality of the music.

For most of us the issue of partnership in the classroom comes down to the problem of control. I suspect that one of the reasons for the popularity of the term *restructuring* is its implication of a new way to control the learning process (or, in gritty reality, to control the kids). It is infinitely simpler to follow a series of predetermined steps with explicit, consequential links than to set out on an adventure in which each stage suggests, rather than determines, the next, and in which each adventurer helps choose the route.

> We split ourselves into controller and controlled. ... This delusion arises from the fact that we speak a language that uses nouns and verbs. Thus we are predisposed to believe that the world consists of things and forces that move the things. But like any living entity, the system of musicians-plus-instruments-plus-listeners-plus-environment is an indivisible, interactive totality; there is something false about splitting it up into parts. (Nachmanovitch, p. 143)

For me it takes a huge leap of faith to give up control in favor of ensemble. My students, sooner or later, want to know if it's really all right to call me Doc. It's a fairly unimaginative nickname that has grown out of their hearing me addressed as Dr. West and being dissatisfied with the distance such formality creates between us. I've never been a first-name teacher, and I frankly admit that it has to do with control. So, I always answer the same way: Sure, you can call me Doc as long as we're friends. For the most part I find that students who don't expect to be friends for long still address me as Dr. West. When they decide it's safe to call me Doc, I know we've accomplished something together. That's as far as I can go right now with that particular power game. Still, I envy my friends whose students confidently refer to them as Sharon and Butch.

I do better when it comes to instructional issues. The one prerequisite for enrolling in Writers' Workshop is to have failed English. It's a great course to teach because there's a sort of what-have-we-got-to-lose feeling about it. I've started conducting class meetings to decide what kinds of writing they'd like to try, and we vote. They choose the major units. As teacher, I get one free choice. We *will* write poetry. A recent group chose short stories, reviews, philosophical essays, and "school writing." Small wonder. They have failed most often at the five-paragraph essay, which they (sadly) believe is the ultimate written form. That's why they are in my class.

Before we leave this subject, I want to clarify the business of audience (Nachmanovitch refers to them as "listeners" because he's talking about music). Not audience for writing, but the real audience for our ensemble work—parents, professional colleagues, administrators. Power (1990) applies the jazz metaphor (Gordon, 1984) to teacher education, and underscores the importance of building our structures outward from the classroom to the institution: Teachers "can improvise in their classrooms, and present their improvisations as works for other teachers and researchers to examine" (Power, p. 185). There is no question that the audience affects the performance. And the more the audience knows about music (or learning), the more actively they will influence our work.

My immediate point, however, is that *our students are not the audience*; they are members of the ensemble. In the perennial talk about charismatic teachers, we refer to those individuals whose personalities strike a chord with some kind of energy in their students. Beginning teachers often see charisma as performance, but it is more than that. Teachers draw students into learning by teaching what they love and by loving to learn. For an ensemble to develop, the patterns must begin to merge — how the teacher learns and what the teacher loves with how students learn and what students love.

Rules and Limits

"The limits are either rules of the game to which we voluntarily accede, or circumstances beyond our control that demand an adaptation" (Nachmanovitch, p. 79). To make sense of this, I have to create a semantic distinction that Nachmanovitch does not intend. Rules are a kind of limit, but rules probably should be seen as structure-making, as form-creating. Rules may have the same function as objectives. Limits, on the other hand, are obstructive realities. Something that we don't get to choose is a limit. Something that we do get to choose is a rule. The fifty-minute class period is a limit. "Students must talk about the title of the story in their responses" is a rule.

Even though I teach Romanticism with an aging hippie's fervor, I have to schedule a writing assignment in the computer lab on Monday and Tuesday or give up my class's turn until the following week. That's a limit. I also want every student to read and discuss at least one poem by each of the five major English Romantic poets. That's a rule.

Some limits are so much a part of our learning structure that we have internalized them. A huge difference between a beginning and an experienced teacher is knowing how long a lesson will take to complete. This knowledge is largely intuitive, is in fact an excellent example of what I mean by intuition: not known by magic but learned through experience, internalized, so that it no longer requires conscious analysis.

Another limit that becomes intuitive with practice is finding the right instructional level. The teacher has a starting point, the old proximal zone. But this limit is assailable. One improvisatory act that occurs in a classroom is the extension of the limit imposed by students' instructional levels. Deciding when to raise the ante is not something that requires planning. We don't say, "Good, you understand that. Now let's keep practicing it until I have time to make a new lesson plan for the next level."

Limits engender growth — or its opposite. This is a structuring issue again. The class is too large. I have too many papers to grade. What is the solution? Learning is pot-bound, strangled in its tangled roots, suffocated by the exhausted soil of drills and whole-class assignments. We tend to meet our limits with more structure, more plans, more handouts—with more limits. I ask myself a simple question. How would I teach this class if I had twenty students and could do it any way I wanted? (If the answer is with drills and worksheets, we are in big trouble.) Is my imagination up to the task? Okay. What, minimally, do I need to change in order to teach a class of thirty-two the same way? Improvise.

Another solution: Pose the problem to the class. Here's what I'd like for us to do. How can we manage to do it? Ensemble improvisation.

Rules, on the other hand, give us a starting point and a context. They are a touchstone. For an ensemble of musicians, says Nachmanovitch, "two rules are more than enough. . . . We can let our imaginations flow freely through the territory mapped out by a pair of rules, confident that the piece will pull together as a definite entity" (pp. 83–84). What two rules are adequate and conducive to learning? Well, the point is that lots of rules are available. We are experts at rules, so we can easily avoid invoking the same two every day. For a writing assignment: In a response of no more than two hundred words (rule one) draw a connection between weather and emotion (rule two). For a class discussion: Write down something that every other student says (rule one), and begin your comments by referring to another student's thoughts (rule two).

Too many rules wreck the ensemble. We begin to listen for the rules only and forget to listen to the music. The time for polishing will come. The day of accountability. Test day. But we're back to the paradox: keep outcomes at bay while we work within the moment. We know how to do this. It's like deferring judgment of our writing, of any art. Imagination shrinks from judgment.

An invitation to the musicians: You be Emily Dickinson and he'll be Walt Whitman. Let's have a conversation. The rest of the class will observe and, after ten minutes, may jump in and ask questions. It's okay if the class is going to write a response to the conversation later; it's even okay if they are going to write essays comparing the two poets. I'm not sure at the beginning where this will go, but I trust that it will lead to thinking about poetry, and I know several ways to guide students in expressing their thoughts. Two rules are enough because I know several ways to operate within those two, and my students will let me know how to help them learn what they need to know.

The point is that classrooms don't have to be rule-bound just because they are crowded. Too many rules means a failure of imagination, a failure of intuition. We have a repertoire of strategies for teaching and learning. So, for that matter, do our students.

Wrestling with the Muse

An artist's inspiration is her muse, but not all muses are solemn and beautiful. Sometimes our greatest inspiration is necessity — the student we can't reach. Nachmanovitch tells of the master craftsman, Antonio Stradivari, who "made some of his most beautiful violins from a pile of broken, waterlogged oars he found on the docks in Venice one day" (p. 87).

At the alternative high school where I teach, the discarded wood comes in the form of teenagers who have all but accepted the official word of the educational community that they are losers and misfits, and who believe in themselves only enough to give it one last try. The music we make requires that our eyes and ears be open to what is largely invisible and silent. We must be sensitive to small successes and celebrate each one. Romano (1991) says that being listened to is "one of the great gifts people can give one another" (p. 4). The results of our sharing this gift can sometimes be quite dramatic, as students like Jeannie begin to listen to their own instruments with doubt and wonder: "Before I came to Open Campus, my dreams for college were going down the drain. Now my goals and dreams are coming back and I hope to have a wonderful future."

Bricolage, says Nachmanovitch, is a French term for "making do with the material at hand" (p. 86). In our classrooms we are masters of bricolage; we have no choice. We make learning out of the human materials at hand. They sometimes surprise us, sometimes seem to be in the way; yet if we are working ensemble, they always contribute to the music. Mistakes and interruptions can stop us cold or they can become part of the pattern. An unexpected dissonance in a jazz improvisation either distracts from the music or changes it in a new direction. What happens when a student says, "I don't know how to do this. This is stupid"? The answer depends on the way the ensemble is working.

Earlier in our conversation, I mentioned play. Nachmanovitch reminds us of the power, in mythology, of "fools, tricksters, holy buffoons" (pp. 46–47). Does this sound at all familiar?

> Trickster is untamed, unpredictable, innocent, sometimes destructive, arising from pre-Creation times, galumphing through life unmindful of past or future, good or evil. Always improvising, unmindful of the consequences of his acts, he may be dangerous; his own experiments often blow up in his face or in others'. But because his play is completely untrammeled ... he is the creator of culture. ... (p. 47).

Perhaps the playful one, the mischief maker, will be the catalyst, not to tear down the pattern but to transform it. The disruptive student in any class can and does affect the music. But there is a positive as well as a negative transformation. We can construct an ensemble that neutralizes (renders invisible) the annoyance or one that includes and engages the trickster. Johnson, Johnson, Holubec, and Roy (1984) describe a group of third-graders who, frustrated by a group member who refuses to come out from under the table, all get down on the floor with him and go on with their work (p. 37).

Forbidden Words

"The artificial separation of work from play ... cleaves our time and the quality of our attention. The attitude of faith says that I and my work are one, and we are organically immanent in one bigger reality" (Nachmanovitch, p. 151). I feel the need for some unabashed use of the words *love*, *faith*, and *commitment*. A bold invocation of *art*. We've rejected some of this because it has been shoved down our throats by people who said we would teach for love and therefore didn't need a reasonable salary. Well, those people aren't welcome in this conversation. Both teaching and learning, when we peel away all the extraneous layers, are acts of love. Our work is play when the ensemble is in tune, when we love the music we are making, when we take inspiration from the ensemble, and when we believe in ourselves and one another.

How far will you go with me in this? History reminds us that great teachers have been wholly committed to learning. Work is not drudgery; it is the practice of our art. Oh, I'll concede that grade books and attendance reports and lunch money are drudgery. Let them have their space, and then let them drop away. When it is time to play, we will sit down together, tune our instruments, acknowledge our limits, and trust the collection of techniques and experiences that each of us brings to the moment. It is possible to see our classrooms this way because we have faith in ourselves. Our intuitions are prepared by a repertoire of ideas, experiences, skills. Our techniques are polished by practice.

It seems only fair to allow Nachmanovitch the penultimate word: "The imagination is our true self, and is in fact the living, creating god within us" (p. 193). If we are to have restructuring (and most of us are), we need to lobby for unstructuring. We already have all kinds of structures, too many rules, not enough intuition, not enough faith. If we can imagine a classroom where learning is a serious and pleasurable activity, where all learners share in the construction of meaning, where surprises are welcomed and incorporated into the music, we have nothing to fear from restructuring. As our ensembles begin to play, we will listen with delight to the exquisite music that our learning makes.

REFERENCES

Gordon, D. (1984). *The myth of schools' self-renewal*. New York: Teachers College Press.

Johnson, D. W., Johnson, R. T., Holubec, E. J., and Roy, P. (1984). *Circles of learning: Cooperation in the classroom*. ASCD.

Mayher, J. S. (1990). *Uncommon sense: Theoretical practice in language education*. Portsmouth, NH: Boynton/Cook.

Nachmanovitch, S. (1990). *Free play: Improvisation in life and art*. Los Angeles: Jeremy P. Tarcher, Inc.

Power, B. M. (1990). Research, teaching, and all that jazz: New metaphors and models for working with teachers. *English Education* **22**, 179–189.

Romano, T. (1991). Writing through others: The necessity of collaboration. In: James L. Collins (Ed.), *Vital signs 2: Teaching and learning language collaboratively* (pp. 3–12). Portsmouth, NH: Heinemann.

Part Two
METHODS

Revising practice is a matter of changing beliefs.
—*Nancy Lester and Cindy Onore*

Reconfiguring the English Classroom for Multiple Intelligences

Peter Smagorinsky
University of Oklahoma

*E*ven in the hands of a teacher committed to the ideals of student-centered education, one who fosters personal expression in writing and discussion and endeavors to enfranchise students through the classroom structure, English classes tend to evaluate students according to their *linguistic* performance. And of course they should, for that is the designated province of Language Arts instruction. The work of Howard Gardner (1975, 1982, 1983, 1984, 1987, and other publications), however, calls this limited avenue of expression into question. Gardner has proposed that *linguistic* intelligence is only one of seven modes of intelligent behavior, only two of which are privileged in American schools: *linguistic* and *logical/mathematical*. Gardner has argued that Binet's concept of "I.Q." has contorted our understanding of how people behave in our society and of what constitutes intelligent behavior. Americans tend to associate a high I.Q. with one's linguistic or logical/mathematical ability, with such figures as the rocket scientist sitting at the intellectual pinnacle as our ideal.

Yet Gardner has argued that rocket scientists and their intellectual kin illustrate only a narrow range of noetic behavior. He gives many examples of people who have been highly valued members of their cultures who would not fare well in American schools or perform well on our intelligence tests. Gardner gives, for instance, the example of sailors who navigate ships at night through an understanding of the configuration of stars and through the recognition of landmarks; we see this skill exhibited in Mark Twain's accounts of Mississippi River navigation and in the performance of the sailors' modern counterpart, the urban cab driver. Gardner maintains that these abilities stem from more than good eyesight, reflexes, and memory: He attributes them to *spatial* intelligence, the ability to perceive the visual spatial world and represent relationships graphically. Others who exhibit spatial intelligence are architects, engineers, artists, billiards players, mechanics, and so on.

Gardner has labeled his theory the "Theory of Multiple Intelligences." The full range of intelligences identified by Gardner includes the following:

1. *Linguistic*: a sensitivity to the sounds, rhythms, and meanings of words and to the different functions of language. Skilled writers, orators, translators, and rap singers (not including Vanilla Ice) are among those with linguistic intelligence.

2. *Logical/mathematical*: a sensitivity to and ability to discern logical or numerical patterns, with the ability to follow or generate long chains of reasoning. Scientists, mathematicians, computer programmers, lawmakers, philosophers, and accountants display logical/mathematical intelligence.

3. *Musical*: the ability to produce and appreciate rhythm, pitch and timbre or to appreciate musical expression. Musicians and music cognoscente possess musical intelligence.

4. *Spatial*: the ability to perceive and represent physical relationships, as demonstrated by graphic artists, newspaper layout specialists, landscapers, and so on.

5. *Bodily/kinesthetic*: the use of the body to solve problems or fashion a product. Note that this is distinct from "physical ability" such as being able to jump high or run fast; rather, it is intelligent expression through physical movement as demonstrated by figure skaters, hunters, and athletes such as the basketball player with good "court sense."

6. *Interpersonal*: the ability to discern or respond appropriately to the moods, temperaments, motivations, and desires of others.

Salespeople, teachers, therapists, and public-relations officers are among those displaying interpersonal intelligence.

7. *Intrapersonal*: the ability to achieve self-knowledge, exhibited by highly reflective individuals and ascetics.

Gardner maintains that only the first two of these intelligences are valued in American schools. We see their privileged status when budgets are cut and art, music, and sports programs are discontinued; we also see this tendency in the dominant classroom structure in which students work silently and individually on the study of personally remote information, with collaboration often regarded as cheating.

Lave's (1988) research on people's extrascholastic thinking illustrates the ways in which schools can discriminate against people whose most effective form of intelligence is not among the most privileged two. He describes, for instance, a participant in a Weight Watchers' class who was measuring quantities of food:

> In this case they were to fix a serving of cottage cheese, supposing the amount laid out for the meal was three-quarters of the two-thirds cup the program allowed. The problem solver in this example began the task muttering that he had taken a calculus course in college. . . . Then after a pause he suddenly announced that he had "got it!" From then on he appeared certain he was correct, even before carrying out the procedure. He filled a measuring cup two-thirds full of cottage cheese, dumped it out on the cutting board, patted it into a circle, marked a cross on it, scooped away one quadrant, and served the rest. . . . At no time did the Weight Watcher check his procedure against a paper and pencil algorithm, which would have produced ¾ cup × ⅔ cup = ½ cup. (p. 165)

The Weight Watcher participant, if given this problem in a math class, would surely have gotten the "wrong" answer. Yet in the practical world of affairs he has succeeded in his own unorthodox way in solving the problem. It appears as if he has used *spatial* intelligence to measure the correct amount of cottage cheese, instead of taking the more common mathematical approach. Such people are often inappropriately labeled as "failures" in school due to their reliance on a form of intelligence that is not recognized by the institution.

Beyond these global problems, the bounds of each discipline tend to be rigidly delineated. Most recommendations for reform do not address the compartmentalized nature of secondary schooling with distinct duties assigned to each discipline. This system works against the abilities of most students, who are not blessed with intelligence in all seven areas, but rather in a few. We see this inequity in the behavior of most people: the successful writer who cannot understand plumbing or tune a car engine, the technically brilliant doctor with a poor "bedside manner," the acclaimed musician who can't handle finances. In most English classes, even those that are consciously student-centered, students are allowed to express themselves almost exclusively in linguistic terms. This leads to problems when students understand literature but express their interpretations poorly through language. Given the opportunity to sculpt a character, compose a soundtrack for a dramatic scene, or act out a character's dilemma, these students might have avenues of expression more suited to their native intelligence.

Remarkably, such means of expression are common and highly valued in the artistic world yet are often disallowed for secondary students. Musicians and choreographers create ballet and modern dance to depict their interpretation of literature. Soundtrack artists are highly compensated in Hollywood for their ability to communicate the mood of a scene. The Disney animators expressed their response to classical compositions with their classic "Fantasia." Artists, musicians, and poets have often created works of enduring value in response to one another's creations, from Gounod's operatic version of *Romeo and Juliet* to A. B. Spellman's poem "John Coltrane" to the myriad artistic renditions of Biblical scenes and stories. Such response, however, is rarely allowed or encouraged in American English classes.

We occasionally see collages, student plays, and illustrated cover pages to book reports, all as laudable as they are infrequent. I have proposed (Smagorinsky, 1991) a reconfiguration of English classes based on the assumption that in a truly student-centered class, students are empowered not only to explore personal responses to literature and choose the content and form of their composition, but to express their ideas and interpretations through their most effective vehicle of intelligence. I am not arguing that English classes should no longer require reading and writing; composition and discussion have traditionally been the meat and potatoes of English classes and I am not suggesting anything so radical as their termination. I am proposing, however, that students be provided with alternatives, perhaps in the form of supplementary opportunities for expression and response. Often students understand material quite well but do poorly on their linguistic evaluations. These students then perceive themselves as academic losers even though they might be quite successful in their personal relations, baby sitting, guitar playing, animal care, automobile maintenance, personal financial management, and so on.

Particularly affected by the narrow range of assessment in American schools are our cultural minorities. Members of minority groups tend to do quite poorly in our schools and are thus often perceived as intellectually inferior. The experience of Spanish-speaking students will illustrate this problem. Steinberg, Blinde, and Chan (1984) have found that native speakers of Spanish have had a distressing and persistently high rate of failure in American schools. Moll (1986, 1988, 1990) attributes this performance not to any inherent intellectual disability of the students, but to entrenched classroom practices that underestimate, undervalue, and constrain the students' means of intellectual expression. American schools, for instance, tend to isolate students for formal evaluation of remote knowledge, without allowing them to construct meaning by using personal knowledge from their own experiences. Moll argues that Spanish-speaking households rarely function alone or in isolation but are connected through complex social networks that transmit knowledge, skills, information, assistance, and cultural values that can potentially inform their school learning. Moll's study of Mexican-American families in Arizona reveals a wide range of problem-finding and problem-solving behavior, including distilling medicine from insects, building and repairing machinery, operating ranches, and creating and performing music. These acts require intelligences that are central to the lives of students yet not valued by their schools. The students thus continue to fail due not to intellectual deficiencies but to the type of behavior evaluated in school.

The expanding cultural diversity of American schools will exacerbate the problem illustrated by the experience of Southwestern Mexican-Americans. Presently, half of the students in California schools are members of linguistic minorities; by the year 2000 about 40 percent of American students will fall in this category (Lloyd-Jones and Lunsford, 1989). One reaction to the diversification of the American population has been to forcefeed Eurocentric values and ways to minorities in the hopes of preserving and perpetuating "American" culture (Hirsch, 1987; Ravitch and Finn, 1987). I would argue that this response is a futile attempt to turn back the clock; that the times are indeed a-changing and that we will be better off for the infusion of new ways of knowing and behaving. Rather than ignoring the gifts brought to our classrooms by children of diverse cultures; rather than failing them for their non-Eurocentric means of expressing understanding and intelligence; rather than relegating them to the lowest economic strata by perpetuating the perception of them as intellectually deficient; rather than hiding our heads in the sand while these children's talents wither, I argue, in company with Gardner, that we need to recognize their intelligence in the modes valued and taught by their cultures and allow them ways to express it in our classes.

English classes — with their natural ties to the arts, their dependence on interaction for greater understanding, their potential for both logical analysis and personal reflection in response and expression — are among the most promising areas of school for expression through multiple intelligences. Central to any response should be the act of *meaning construction*: Students' expression should signify the manner in which they have reconstructed the problem to which they are responding and illustrate their representation of it.

Teachers can allow opportunities for expression through multiple intelligences in a variety of ways. (See Smagorinsky, 1991, for detailed descriptions of a broad range of activities.) In some cases, teachers can allow students optional supplements to activities that are already in place. Let's take the old English-class warhorse, the research paper. This assignment is often a task in which the students' personal involvement gets lost in the overwhelming new information regarding proper reference-citation form (an issue even with the transition to more user-friendly forms such as APA and MLA) and procedures (finding sources, preparing note cards and so on, many of which may soon become obsolete in their present form with new technologies becoming available). A number of educators have come up with alternatives to the traditional research paper, such as Ken Macrorie's "I-Search" (1988) and W. Keith Kaus' (1978) suggestions for bizarre topics, to make this project interesting and meaningful for students. The emphasis for such papers remains, however, in the realms of linguistic and logical/mathematical intelligence.

Students can have options for the preparation and presentation of their research that enable them to bring into play other types of intelligence. Most topics, for instance, are amenable to some form of interview. Given a choice of topics, many students select personal or contemporary subjects that interest them. A student who has been adopted might research adoption procedures. A Jewish student might research a particular Jewish tradition. The son or daughter of a Vietnam veteran might research some aspect of the conflict. Students might research a musician whose career they have followed, or a problem that threatens teenage life such as drug use or anorexia. Typically the research for such topics takes place in the library with sources found in a print medium. Yet students can gather and present information in unconventional ways. They can, for instance, interview someone who has knowledge related to their topic, such as a Vietnam veteran, a cocaine user or counselor, or the head of an adoption agency. This activity enables them to use interpersonal intelligence. One who has skill at understanding the moods and needs of others can draw out stories that will bring vitality to an informational paper and take advantage of an ability that ordinarily goes unappreciated.

Students can use their spatial intelligence to produce art or photography to illustrate concepts uncovered during research. Students can prepare a slide show or video or computer presentation to share their research with their classmates, perhaps accompanied by a soundtrack that the student either prepares personally or assembles from other sources. In this way the researcher's report can take on the form of a documentary, with the student acting as author/director as well as writer.

In addition to using multiple intelligences to supplement regular activities, students can engage in optional activities that extend their understanding of what they cover in class. Highly reflective individuals, for instance, can keep a journal to record their personal responses to literature and issues and provide an outlet for their intrapersonal intelligence. Students can use these ruminations as the basis for other optional activities. Let's say, for instance, that a student is reading S. E. Hinton's *The Outsiders* and reflects at length on experiences involving clashes between peer groups of different socioeconomic status. The student wishes to express these feelings to classmates in light of other literature they are reading regarding peer-group behavior. The student might assemble a group of friends from class to dramatize a personal experience that parallels those of the literary characters. The group prepares a script for the play and begins to conceive its production. One student is reticent about performing but owns an inexpensive portable synthesizer and decides to provide a theme song and soundtrack. Other students elect to play minor roles but also contribute by creating sets for the production. Another student, hesitant to perform but eager to participate, volunteers to videotape the performance.

This activity involves the coordination of a variety of individuals through a range of intelligences. The original reflection that inspires the play is a result of intrapersonal intelligence. The students all bring interpersonal intelligence to the project in order to engage fruitfully in the group effort. Producing the script requires linguistic intelligence, the soundtrack and theme song require musical intelligence. Several of the contributors use their spatial intelligence: those who create the sets, the person who operates the videocamera, and the person who directs the action. And bodily/kinesthetic intelligence is required of the performers who must use their bodies to convey attitudes and personalities through their stances and gestures.

We see in this sort of activity a reflection of the ways in which individuals tend to perform outside school: they are collaborating on an activity of their choice to construct meaning through personal expression. Different group members contribute different talents to create an effective whole, one that none of the group members could have achieved individually. They are able to benefit from and learn from one another's unique gifts and contributions to participate in an important activity that represents an expression of their understanding of the experiences of literary characters.

These activities illustrate in some detail ways in which teachers can structure classrooms to enable students to express themselves through unconventional avenues of intelligence. I wish to stress again that I do not wish to displace the traditional emphasis on linguistic ability in the English class, but to allow students opportunities to signify their understanding and awareness when their linguistic skills are limited. Teachers can organize their classes so that students can have frequent opportunities for application of unconventional types of intelligence without departing from their established curriculum. Students can engage in frequent informal reflective writing in response to literature and issues, thus employing their intrapersonal intelligence. Teachers can arrange the class to allow for frequent small-group work that enables the use of interpersonal intelligence: for prewriting planning sessions, for group composing (as in script writing or working through the process of a new type of composition), for peer-group response to compositions, and for literary discussions.

Students can use their spatial intelligence to draw, paint, or sculpt literary characters or terrains, photograph relevant scenes (i.e., a desolate cityscape to illustrate the setting for *Native Son* or a bucolic countryside to depict themes of Romanticism), or create sets for dramatic productions. They can respond to literature by creating a musical interpretation (as in Simon and Garfunkel's version of "Richard Cory" or Ralph Towner's instrumental "Icarus"), by creating an original song for a text along the lines of the theme song for "Laura" or countless other films, by adapting an existing musical work as a theme song for literature (such as the borrowing of Pachelbel's "Canon in D Major" for the film *Ordinary People*), or by providing a soundtrack for a dramatic production. And students can use bodily/kinesthetic intelligence for a variety of types of productions; while they needn't necessarily produce Broadway-style musicals or perform Kabuki versions of plays, they still require physical expression to execute roles in simple classroom productions, and for the dexterity required in artistic expression and projects involving construction.

Most suggestions for engendering student-centered classrooms have had the interests of students at heart. I would argue that we should extend them even further, broadening our notion of what is acceptable for evaluation in English classes. We have the examples of master artists who quite naturally construct meaning for themselves and fashion inspiring products for their public by creating original expression or responding to one another's work; if we regard this as a legitimate means of expression for them, then we should certainly approve of it for our students.

REFERENCES

Gardner, H. (1975). *The shattered mind.* New York: Knopf.

——— (1982). *Art, mind and brain.* New York: Basic Books.

——— (1983). *Frames of mind.* New York: Basic Books.

——— (1984). The seven frames of mind. *Psychology Today*, June, 21–26.

——— (1986). The development of symbolic literacy. In M. Wrolstad and D. Fisher (Eds.), *Toward a greater understanding of literacy.* New York: Praeter.

——— (1987). The theory of multiple intelligences. *Annals of Dyslexia 37*, 12–35.

Hirsch, E. D. (1987). *Cultural literacy.* Boston: Houghton Mifflin.

Kaus, W. K. (1978). *Murder, mischief and mayhem.* Urbana, IL: NCTE.

Lave, J. (1988). *Cognition in practice.* Boston, MA: Cambridge.

Lloyd-Jones, R., and Lunsford, A. (1989). *The English coalition conference: Democracy through language.* Urbana, IL: NCTE; New York: MLA.

Macrorie, K. (1988). *The I-search paper.* Portsmouth, N.H.: Boynton/Cook.

Moll, L. (1986). Writing as communication: Creating strategic learning environments for students. *Theory Into Practice 25*(2), 102–108.

——— (1988). Key issues in teaching Latino students. *Language Arts 65*(5), 465–472.

——— (1990). Literacy research in community and classrooms: A socio-cultural approach. Paper presented at the conference on "Multi-disciplinary Perspectives on Research Methodology in Language Arts," NCRE, February 16–18, Chicago.

Ravitch, D., and Finn, C. (1987). *What do our seventeen-year-olds know?.* New York: Harper and Row.

Smagorinsky, P. (1991). *Expressions: Multiple intelligences in the English class*. Urbana, IL: NCTE.

Steinberg, L., Blinde, P. L., and Chan, K. (1984). Dropping out among minority youth. *Review of Educational Research 54*, 113–132.

Trying to Understand Together: Restructuring Classroom Talk About Texts

Suzanne Miller
State University of New York at Albany

I still remember that moment twenty years ago when I read my next day's lesson plans with sudden bewilderment: "Ninth grade—discuss essay." What did I mean by that? I wondered. It had slipped easily onto the page, I'm sure—the sort of thing I'd heard my English teachers say for years. Yet trying to detail that fourth-day-ever of teaching my own classes startled me with latent problems. How does a teacher start discussion? How would I keep it going? What did I want students to say and do—really? And why? The content of that day's lesson has faded, but ever since I have been turning these questions over in my mind.

Studies of typical classroom talk provided no clue: teachers tend to ask questions and evaluate student answers for correctness. I wanted more from discussion—I wanted *students* to question and evaluate, to interpret and justify. I have talked to teachers who believe that discussion only works rarely with a magic combination of people. And I have read about students exploring text responses together in small teacherless groups — which failed when their social and cognitive limitations interfered. When I had the chance to observe how high-school teachers trained in discussion used open-ended discussion of essays in their urban classes, I learned how they restructure classroom talk to encourage thinking.

Critical Thinking as Dialogue

In theory, discussion provides a rich occasion for critical thinking. The most compelling views of critical thinking portray it as an inclination to raise questions about and evaluate the grounds for our own and others' beliefs, claims, and interpretations (Cornbleth, 1985; Dewey, 1933; McPeck, 1981); equally important, though, critical thinking has its source in our interpretive and evaluative response to what we encounter in the world as we cast our understanding into our own language to become conscious of and learn to examine what we know (Bakhtin, 1981; Bartholomae and Petrosky, 1986; Petrosky, 1984). Taken together, these ideas point not only to the skeptical, questioning nature of critical thinking, but also to its constructive meaning-making nature. Critical thinking, then, can usefully be seen as internalized dialogue where the mind takes both parts: generating responses, ideas, explanations *and* listening skeptically, to question and challenge, to provoke and weigh justification (Bakhtin, 1981; Friere, 1970; Tough, 1977; Vygotsky, 1962, 1978).

Such thinking does not occur by "spontaneous combustion," Dewey (1933) argues, or "just on 'general principles.' There is something that occasions or evokes it" (p. 15). Through discussion we can make our responses and ideas available for ourselves and others, with the distinctive benefit of setting several perceptions of the matter under discussion alongside one another, challenging our own view of things with those of others (Bridges, 1979). As students' thinking becomes "visible" in talk, it becomes subject to questioning and challenging through the pull of others' talk. Unexamined perspectives are thrown into relief against alternatives, dramatizing the need to evaluate the conflicting ways of interpreting the world (Bakhtin, 1981; Friere, 1967; Gadamer, 1976). Discussion is uniquely suited to evoke the inclination to think critically, then, because awareness of one's point of view as one among many can occasion a state of doubt that spurs examination of evidence and reasons (Dewey, 1933). Theoretically, this interpersonal classroom dialogue can move inward to become intrapersonal, the internal dialogue of critical thinking (Vygotsky, 1962, 1978).

But how can a teacher initiate this dialogue in a classroom? Students I interviewed about their roles in class discussions I had taped felt their teachers' behaviors were most important in creating the "environment" for discussion. Linda M.'s ninth-grade college-bound students, for instance, credited her with helping them change from their initial "debate attitude" to an inclination to consider the grounds for alternative views. In what follows, I sketch how Linda M. restructured classroom talking to encourage students both to generate responses and to question them. Then, I examine the powerful roles of alternative perspectives and student-initiated questions in provoking student thinking.

Transforming Roles and Responsibilities

Linda's primary discussion goal was for her eleven Anglo, ten African-American, and four Asian students to develop a "sense of community" so they could try to understand the different perspectives she expected would emerge in their class. To introduce discussion, Linda knew she must first change students' attitudes: rather than looking to her for right answers she wanted students to turn to one another for possibilities. The challenge, she saw, was to "teach them *how to discuss* — to listen and cooperate." To this end, she signaled a changed context and new roles through her consistent behaviors. She put the desks in a "tight circle" where students could see and hear one another and took a seat in the circle. She selected strong texts open to interpretation, changed to informal, nonevaluative language (e.g., "I'm kinda confused"), and opened discussion with questions about what in the texts puzzled her. Linda's rule for herself was to "wait and allow them to say it the way that they say it." She listened to students, talking herself on an average of only 17 percent of the turns. She allowed long pauses for "thinking time." As she suggested to another teacher who wondered about how to keep discussion going, Linda let students talk and eventually a difference of opinion emerged "and that prompts discussion of itself."

Yet, some students I interviewed in her class said at first they felt "afraid to talk" and just observed to see "what was normal." To create dialogue among students who (like most) had never had that opportunity in a classroom, Linda patiently helped them learn new behaviors. For example, she insisted on student responsibility to listen considerately.

For one thing, that meant she enforced social listening behaviors as explicit ground rules (e.g., "Do not interrupt") and provided and modeled strategies, such as "Look at the speaker" (on videotape it is evident that heads turn when speakers change). In over a quarter of her turns she reminded students of guidelines at points of need (e.g., "No side talking—share with the class"), which students saw as helping to create a "serious purpose" and "a good attitude" for discussion.

Even so, Linda felt students at first generated opinions lined up as "isolated pronouncements"; she saw that they needed to learn new cognitive behaviors as well, such as questioning one another and challenging respectfully. To teach this responsive aspect of considerate listening, Linda encouraged students to enter intellectually into the dialogue: for instance, she modeled asking speakers for clarification ("So are you saying . . . ?") and provided procedural explanations and metaphors for collaborative response (e.g., respond so meaning "builds and grows").

As students moved from fear of discussion to a considerate atmosphere for speaking and listening, their thinking was transforming as well, toward an open-minded tentativeness that inclined the group to reflect about alternatives. In second-semester discussions, more students took on Linda's careful ways of talking, tending to own their claims ("I think that what he's saying . . ."), state them tentatively ("Maybe not, maybe it's . . ."), and propose possibilities ("Could it mean that . . . ?"). Over time students learned to respond to and consider views different from their own. Jack, for example, attributed his and other students' learning to talk "*with* each other" rather than "*at* each other" to Linda's persistent support.

Students felt the class develop into a "safe group" where they had authority to express and elaborate their responses *and* the responsibility to listen to and consider alternatives. On an average, almost two-thirds of the students participated in any given discussion, including several who said they didn't "open up" to talk in other classes where students didn't listen or the teacher looked for particular answers. Only one painfully shy student, who told me she loved to listen, never participated, and varying students played major roles in different discussions. Linda's attention to social and cognitive behaviors *both*, I believe, led to her success in restructuring her classroom talk for discussion. As students embraced the social-cognitive purpose that Linda determinedly communicated—"Try to understand together"—they came to see their class as a community with what her student Antoine dubbed "the right atmosphere for discussion."

Arousing Thinking Through the Dialogue of Alternatives

In this classroom context where perspectives interplayed, students explored possibilities, creating an atmosphere of reflection, "a ferment of interpretive activity" (Bruner, 1985). Increasingly, students collaborated to question the text and one another, initiate interpretations, provide personal and textual evidence, and explain reasons. In their twenty-second weekly discussion, about a two-page excerpt from the philosopher Pascal's *Pensées* translated for use in high school (Comber, Maistrellis, O'Grady, and Zeiderman, 1985), students exhibited all these indicators of critical thinking more than ever before.

The discussion illustrates how being caught up in purposeful dialogue of alternatives stimulated student thinking. No grades were at stake, no one was called on to speak. But in proposing rival possibilities, each student posed a problem—that which "perplexes and challenges the mind so that it makes belief at all uncertain" (Dewey, 1933, p. 13). The revelation of these different opinions was the surprise and lure of discussion, students said, the motivation for talking and thinking. Excerpts from the discussion printed below highlight the intellectual and emotional intensity possible among a group of 14- 15-year-olds in this encouraging context. The exact words of their interplaying languages— the moving back and forth from what they knew, to what others knew, to what the text seemed to know—bring to light the earnestness of their thinking, what Linda called their "sincerity."

Linda selected Pascal's essay for discussion because she felt the topic would engage students and be difficult enough to compel them to turn to one another for understanding. The text begins by describing "even as children" what "we are told" will make us happy—health, reputation, money. It goes on to portray such people who pursue only these things and "have to keep busy" for they find that "to think about what they are, where they come from, and where they are going . . . [is] unbearable." The piece ends by sharply calling to question all that has come before—"Isn't such a person's heart empty and ugly?"

Their longest collaborative sequence began when Linda read aloud the text lines about people staying busy to avoid thinking and then responded, "That part bothered me." She often modeled such expressive response to the text, vague feelings that seemed to invite sharing the personal experience of reading as a starting point for an interpretive/evaluative dialogue. Julie answered, "It's true," and Linda probed briefly, conversationally, "It's true?" Darla responded to explain, seeming to think out loud, and concluded with the qualification that "some people can't handle" thinking about themselves. In the turns that followed students generated different perspectives about *which* people feel this way, pursuing this implicit question that spurred their thinking.

Transcribed from audiotape, this talk frozen as text may look strange, with its repetitions and false starts, but it captures some of the sound of thinking aloud, the interplay of response and reasoning. Antoine elaborated his agreement with Darla:

> *(1) Antoine*: That's absolutely true. If you like stop right now and think, "What am I gonna do? Where am I going? What's my future?" I mean nobody knows it. I mean, if you haven't been that great, you probably could have been the richest person in the world right now if you had just [unclear]. Right now I don't know what I'm going to be. I could be a bum in ten years or I could be wealthy. I could be anything. But if you just keep on doing what you are doing, you have no time to think about that, and you just do what you have to do, and that's that. But if you stop and think, you get depressed. "Could be a junkie in ten years." But if, but if you just do what has to be done and keep busy, play sports, whatever, write newspapers, just do something and—[he stops].

> *(2) Linda*: Dave, you've been waiting.

> *(3) Dave*: I agree that that is true, for a lot, maybe even most people, but some people make themselves aware of themselves. They know what they are going to do ten years from now, and they, they just say, "Tomorrow I'm going to do this," and it doesn't bother them. They need to know what they are doing and such. They got to know a lot about themselves, just to keep themselves, that's the way they keep themselves stable. I think this entire piece is speaking of a particular person and his happiness. I don't think you can say how one person can be happy and how another person can be happy.

> *(4) Darla*: 'Cause everybody is different and you don't know how everybody feels, how everybody thinks about something. You all could have a different point of view from everybody in this class and I don't think, you know, I guess you can, in a way, just generalizing, but if you want to really get down to it, I don't think you can say, because everybody is different.

> *(5) Ivan*: But he's talking generally. Just like you, your friends, say about boys, "They all act alike." Right?

In response to the idea that bothers Linda, Antoine (#1) gives his thinking a voice ("What's my future?") to give his examples authority ("to get his point across," he told me) and suggests that they all are faced with an uncertain future ("Could be a junkie in ten years"). His examples have a personal quality to them (Linda saw his city "environment" reflected here), and with such worries it is best, he concludes, to keep busy. He weighs his personal experience in the world against this perspective, providing evidence and explanation to extend the argument.

Linda (playing a typical procedural role) provides an opening for Dave (#2) and he (#3) finds common ground: "That is true, for a lot, maybe even most people." Yet he sees an opposing view: "but some people make themselves aware of themselves." He has listened to Antoine's comments closely and answers, point by point (e.g., "in ten years . . ."), to structure his argument about other people planning to remain "stable." Considering both what Antoine knows and what *he* knows about people, Dave tries out a new reading of the text: it cannot apply to everyone, so it must be "speaking of a particular person and his happiness."

Darla (#4) continues Dave's thought by adding evidence based on what she knows of the class—that they have different points of view. She seems to have been swayed by Dave's argument and suggests a limited value in "just generalizing," providing this new word to help them think about who this text refers to. Ivan (#5), though, maintains that the author must be speaking "generally," drawing on his own experience with people "generalizing."

Shortly after, Dave revised his reading, using the word Darla and Ivan together have provided: "What I was trying to say is you can't speak about happiness in a *general* sense because everyone's happiness is different." Darla agreed with this more explicit view that Dave then related to the text:

> *(19) Dave*: He's [Pascal] being very specific about how you have to be happy. You have to have good reputation and your friends have to have good reputation, and money in the bank and so forth. And you have to be busy and stuff like that to be happy. But I have to think that you cannot say, "If you are going to be happy you do this, if you are going to be happy you have to do that." You have to do whatever makes you happy. You can't just be too general. [two-second pause]
>
> *(20) Michelle*: I don't know. I'm not sure. I don't think this is talking about one specific person because everybody has doubts about themselves. But then again, no one, I don't know anyone who really hates themselves. And although there is a lot of different things that make people happy, those things usually are, at least one thing, you know, if a person has to write one thing from a list of things, I'm sure that at least one of those things [health, money, reputation] is going to be on their list. So I don't think it's talking about one specific person. I don't think a person needs all these things to be happy. But sooner or later one of those things is going to come up. [three-second pause]

Dave clarifies (#19) his reading by translating what he sees as the text argument, using the word "specific" to counterpoint the word "generally" other students are working with. In terms parallel to the text wording, he opposes the text, providing support for his disagreement. From his transactions with the text and other students, then, Dave is now able to explain that this recipe for happiness is what he finds "too general." He, instead, locates happiness within the individual ("whatever makes you happy").

In the final turn in this collaborative sequence, Michelle begins in a tone of puzzling out, connecting her disagreement directly to Dave's words which have prompted her thinking: "I don't think this is talking about one *specific* person." She considers what the group has said, what Dave has said, and what she knows to introduce a larger perspective to include these points of view — a way to accept Dave's new formulation that people are happy in different ways, while acknowledging that the ways people are happy are not all different. Differences in views of happiness, as in views of a text, do not imply that there is nothing in common.

Throughout this fairly typical sequence students cast the text into their own expressive terms, producing opposing interpretations that dramatized the individual's need to justify for the group. Because rival possibilities are at issue, students examine the personal and textual bases of their responses, provide and provoke evidence and explanation, challenge with new possibilities. As students perceived a new basis for knowing, grounded not in teacher evaluation of correctness but in their own weighing of the justifications for their beliefs, the inclination to think critically developed out of the dialogue of alternatives.

Valuing Puzzlement in Student initiated-Inquiry

Students felt their authority to think critically in discussion most keenly as they initiated their own questions about the text. A favorite story students told in the interviews concerned a frustrated Antoine calling out before discussion, "I don't understand what Descartes is saying, can someone explain this to me?" Linda, showing her typical sensitivity to opportunities for thinking, made that the opening question, and the group responded by collaborating on interpretations "to help each other understand." Not knowing and being puzzled became valued and welcome in the class. As Jack put it, "It's everybody's questions that keep discussion going." The power of student questions to provoke thinking and collaborative learning was evident in the conclusion to the Pascal discussion.

Shortly after the sequence described above, Julie returned to the words of the text to raise a question that she told me she had been asking herself all during the discussion:

> There is one sentence I don't understand in this. . . . In the second paragraph, the last sentence. "Isn't such a person's heart empty and ugly?" After you read that, the paragraph, I don't understand how he [Pascal] can say that. I wanted somebody to explain to me how, how it can be empty? [ten-second pause]

Reading the transcript later, Linda said here, "We have the biggest pause of all because that's a hard question. That was real pivotal to the discussion." This was the kind of moving back to the text to question that Linda herself had often modeled. Jack told me this question "made me think." Julie's confusion posed a dilemma for them all. Note that in the turns that follow, this question to be answered "holds the current of ideas to a definite channel" (Dewey, 1933, p. 14), prompting students to form answers over successive turns of talk. What may not be so readily evident is the quickening that the question brought, energizing the talk in a way that was different in kind from the rest.

Jack searched for a solution to the discrepancy Julie pointed to by returning to the text he had been rejecting because of its definition of happiness. In this response he revises his reading of the text, recomposing the parts that have been discussed, for the first time justifying his perspective:

> He had an ugly heart because he thinks he's above everybody else because he's rich and had good friends and all that. And he thinks he's better than everybody else. I mean the evidence comes from the fact that he never really did think about who he is because he just kept going because of what his parents said. Never really looked at himself and said, "Where am I going? Or where did I come from?" They [empty and ugly] just both go together if you never did that, never thought about yourself.

Provoked by Julie's question, he now marshalls evidence from the text to support and expand his initial feeling that an individual's view of happiness is more important than, as he said earlier, "how other people see you." He returns to the question of keeping busy, concluding that never asking himself "Where am I going?" makes this character empty and ugly. Using the character as a negative example, Jack translates the text as arguing *for* the value of thinking. He is the first to suggest that this advice in the text comes from the voices a person hears, from "parents," not from Pascal. Perplexity spurred Jack to search for solutions, and he found a supportable one in the idea that more than one perspective about happiness interplayed in the text.

Ma Ling, who reported in an interview that she all along had been responding silently and urging herself to talk, was drawn in by Julie's question and Jack's new reading and spoke next to argue a related view of the text, but in her own terms:

> I understand why people want to spend free time keeping busy . . . why people are not happy to, I mean, when they are thinking about themselves. Um, by thinking themselves and [unclear] they can, they will be getting real happiness from thinking. I think that, um, um, good friend and good health and good reputation and a lot of money are um, are all the factors that contribute to man's happiness. Um, I think we do need something more to be happy. Um, as well as money and health and reputations. Um, and I do think also this author, Pascal, um, also a thinker, he did a lot of thinking, and through thinking, he got real happiness.

Ma ling takes up threads from previous sequences in the discussion, accepting what she can of the efforts of previous collaborations, point by point (e.g., "keeping busy"). The more inclusive view she argues is that friends, health, reputation, and wealth contribute to happiness, but "we do need something more to be happy." She has reconstituted the themes of the discussion and placed them in a new perspective that acknowledges them, but adds on another point of view, the view of "a thinker" for whom thinking brought "real happiness."

This view is one that Ivan told me he did not understand—"I couldn't relate her statement to me." Consider that this conversation about philosophically different world views between Ivan, a popular African-American male in the class, and Ma Ling, a female newly arrived from China, was not likely to occur of its own in the school hallways. Because of the habits of mind developing in the class, Ivan's puzzlement prompted him to probe further, in effect prodding Ma Ling to explain her ideas:

> (1) *Ivan*: Um, when you said, what do you do with your free time?
>
> (2) *Ma Ling*: Thinking and sometimes doing "sports and hobbies," but I do take time to think about herself. [quote from the text]
>
> (3) *Ivan*: Okay, now he says, in order to be happy, do you always think about yourself?
>
> (4) *Ma Ling*: Not always, sometimes. Frequently I think about myself.
>
> (5) *Ivan*: Do you make free time to think about yourself? You might

have some [unclear], but he's saying something different. I think what he's saying is when he has free time, he tries not to make time to think about himself. You do. So.

(6) Ma Ling: I think the thinking is very important to happiness.

(7) Ivan: Uh, you think about problems?

(8) Ma Ling: Yes.

(9) Ivan: Sometimes you can become depressed thinking about—

(10) Ma Ling: You can solve problems by thinking! Pascal was a thinker and he did a lot of thinking. More than anyone else. Ummm. [four-second pause]

(11) Julie: So you are saying work to solve your problems, we can't ignore them, we have to think about them in order to solve them.

(12) Ma Ling: Yeah, uh-hmmm.

(13) Julie: So while we're thinking we'll find answers to these problems—

Ma Ling responds to Ivan's questions, searching for her answers sometimes (#2, 4, 6, 8). Ivan tries out a tentative reading that distinguishes between Ma Ling's view of thinking and Pascal's (#5). When he begins to return to Antoine's previous point about thinking causing depression (#9), Ma Ling, more assertive than ever before (#10), suggests for the first time that thinking is a kind of action, too: "You can solve problems by thinking!" Julie (#11) tests out her understanding of Ma Ling's point and, then, extends this new idea in a tone of dawning awareness—thinking can lead to "answers" (#13).

Ivan, now puzzled by the text, questions why, if Pascal "takes time" to think, would he write "people should always have hobbies so they wouldn't think"? This question sparks another realization for Jack. In his "Wait a second," he is coming to a new understanding of the text problem he has been pursuing all along:

> Wait a second! He's talking about a lot of people tell you this, but he totally disagrees with this in the last sentence. "Isn't such a person's heart empty and ugly?" He disagrees with what everybody else is saying about how other people, about how you should always be healthy and have a lot of friends and be rich. He doesn't agree with that.

His reading is more explicit than before; he uses the words of the text to illustrate and support his understanding of the opposing perspectives he sees there that are causing Ivan problems. In the conclusion that he draws, Jack interprets how the parts of the text relate: Pascal talks about how "some people tell you this" but "he totally disagrees with this in the last sentence." During the discussion Jack had pushed against others' interpretations and continued to return to others' thinking to sharpen his own, but the tension of Julie's and Ivan's questions provoked his revised reading, a supported interpretation recombining text elements he had overlooked at first.

A few turns later, Mei Won, a native Chinese speaker who had never spoken in twenty-two discussions, said softly, "I have something to tell about the last sentence." Linda quietly encouraged her to speak, and she said:

> I read the last sentence, "A man is a thinking being." Human being must think about something . . . Only human being have the ability of thinking, but many people try to avoid from thinking themselves because [The bell rings. No one moves.] because, um, every person, every people are not perfect, so they are afraid to think about they are not perfect. They always keep the fear. So I think the person who always keep busy, is, uh, don't have time to think about something, so their heart is "empty and ugly."

When Mei Won finished speaking, there was a long, appreciative silence, and slowly students began closing their books, murmuring to each other. In her comments she has translated elements from the text to support her interpretation. Most compelling, perhaps, is her explanation of that evidence — she names the culprit as fear, putting "not thinking" in a less favorable light than others had. She relates her example back to what others had said, but also explains that such people are "empty and ugly" *because* they are acting out of fear and avoiding the human ability to think.

There was a sense as students began to leave, after Mei Won spoke, of coming out of a trance, coming back to reality. They were slow to move and they seemed to feel, as I did, as Linda did, that we all had been carried away by something remarkable. Gadamer contends that genuine conversation "embraces the persons playing . . . and the very fascination of the game for the playing consciousness roots precisely in its being taken up into a movement that has its own dynamic . . . the individual player participates in full earnest, when he no longer holds himself back as one who is merely playing" (1978, p. 66). As statement and counterstatement interplayed in this and other discussions, this attitude of being absorbed, being borne along that also marks the hold of a question on the mind — "it holds and buoys up the mind and gives an onward impetus to thinking" (Dewey, 1933, p. 32) — seemed to take hold of the group.

Julie told me, yes, her question that began the sequence had been answered, and "You know what I think is really neat? When Mei Won sums up at the end. She just listens and then summarizes and answers the question." This appreciation of Mei Won's interpretation was widespread. Having Mei Won speak at length seemed to represent their group's success in learning how to talk and think together. Their group ways of indwelling in a provoking question and of respectfully considering alternatives allowed her, finally, to feel she had the authority to speak and contribute to the meaning they were making.

Valuing Discussion

How do we judge the worth of such discussion? Perhaps their conclusions could more efficiently have been transmitted through lecture. What's to be gained from taking the time to discuss? Or the time to look so closely at the talk?

These students raised and pursued questions in ways I have rarely seen in the secondary school. In the interplay of opposing points of view, they talked to try to understand together, composing readings of the essay and the world from the languages made available in the text and in discussion, learning to question and justify beliefs to authorize meanings. Once they felt the pull of other perspectives, they were roused to intellectual curiosity, stimulated to a purposeful wholeheartedness that Dewey (1933) long ago recognized as centrally important to intellectual development.

These were not rare and magical ninth-graders. They were a rather typical mix of young teens in an urban school who learned new social-cognitive behaviors and attitudes from their teacher for a real purpose. Listening to other students and considering their ideas became purposeful activities only when, in the drama of rival possibilities, students trusted that Linda did not have right answers waiting in the wings, that the texts and the ideas really were open to their interpretations and questions, evaluations and answers. As students felt authorized to use personal language to explore their thinking, they took the risk of involvement in discussion. The group's diversity, gaps in understanding, puzzlements were not treated as educational problems or failures, but were valued as providing the compelling purpose for discussion and thinking.

Linda's "willingness to give up control" of topics and interpretations did not leave her passively out of work. Without her active restructuring of the talk—redefining roles, constantly "reading" her students to provide new strategies at the moments when they needed them—I think nothing new would have happened. In many ways, hers was the star performance. She admired students finding the courage to speak, but just as admirable was her courage in redefining who she was in the class, so her students could learn to do more than they could have alone. I believe the changed character of the group resulted from this sensitive teacher persistently modeling, encouraging, supporting new social-cognitive behaviors—responding and explaining, listening and questioning. Her careful "messages" about the changing context and her eager listening to the diverse views her students composed provide starting points for all of us who have long wondered how to restructure our classroom talk to encourage thinking.

The story of this class learning to discuss suggests the combined power of a supportive teacher and collaborating students to create the context for and arouse the dialogue of critical thinking. Linda challenged and supported students *and* created ways for students to challenge and support one another, to transform themselves through discussion. Students found themselves attending to their own and others' language, initiating questions, sustaining inquiry along a path of their own making. They found themselves reading, not "to absorb" for tests, but to respond and question, "to make your own opinion" for discussion. It seems fitting that in our increasingly diverse nation, students learn this *inclination* to listen to those with opposing views, to question ideas, to generate and weigh justifications—particularly in English classrooms, where discussing texts to develop literate thinking has been, I suspect, our goal all along.

Alfred North Whitehead argued in *Aims of Education*:

> Knowledge does not keep any better than fish. You may be dealing with knowledge of the old species, with some old truth; but somehow or other it must come to the students, as it were, just drawn out of the sea and with the freshness of its immediate importance (cited in Berthoff, 1981, p. 134).

When students engaged with that old idea, as Mei Won put it, "A man is a thinking being," that came to them "new" as they created it themselves, drawing it out of the sea of their own experiences and the languages of the text and of discussion. The "freshness of its immediate importance," I believe, developed most keenly as they tested its personal importance in word and deed, questioning and justifying that conclusion with absorbed interest, by acting as thinkers. Julie explained how she had changed: "There are so many points of view about things. I've learned so much. I go home and think about it. I go home and ask my dad what he thinks about the texts. We talk about it, and I see where we agree and disagree." As Julie and the others came to see themselves as thinkers, for whom thinking was a positive action, they awakened to their capacity for reflection, to a questioning spirit.

REFERENCES

Bakhtin, M. (1981). *The dialogic imagination*. (C. Emerson and M. Helquist, Trans.). Austin, TX: University of Texas Press.

Bartholomae, D., and Petrosky, A. (1986). *Facts, artifacts and counterfacts: Theory and method for a reading and writing course*. Portsmouth, NH: Boynton/Cook.

Berthoff, A. E. (1981). *The making of meaning*. Portsmouth, NH: Boynton/Cook.

Bridges, D. (1979). *Education, democracy and discussion*. Windsor, England: NFER.

Comber, G., Maistrellis, N., O'Grady, W., and Zeiderman, H. (Eds. and Trans.). (1985). *Touchstones: Texts for discussion* (2nd ed.). Annapolis: C Z M Press.

Cornbleth, C. (1985). Critical thinking and cognitive processes. In W. B. Stanley (Ed.), *Review of research in social studies education: 1976–1983*. Washington, DC: National Council for the Social Studies.

Dewey, J. (1933). *How we think: A restatement of the relation of reflective thinking to educative process*. Boston, MA: D. C. Heath.

Friere, P. (1970). *Pedagogy of the oppressed* (M. Bergman Ramos, Trans.). New York: The Seabury Press.

Gadamer, H. (1976). *Philosophical hermeneutics* (D. Linge, Ed. and Trans.). Berkeley, CA: University of California Press.

McPeck, J. E. (1981). *Critical thinking and education*. Oxford: Martin Robertson.

Petrosky, A. R. (1984, October). *What it means to teach critical thinking in the schools*. Paper presented at The Conference on Critical Thinking, Kingsborough Community College of the City University of New York.

Tough, J. (1977). *Talking and learning*. London: Ward Lock.

Vygotsky, L. S. (1962). *Thought and language*. (E. Hanfmann and G. Vakar, Eds. and Trans.). Cambridge, MA: The M.L.T. Press.

——— (1978). *Mind in society: The development of higher psychological processes*. Cambridge, MA: Harvard University Press.

Crossing Boundaries: Teaching About Cultural Stereotypes

Diane D. Brunner
Michigan State University

I didn't know I was poor until ninth grade. It was the third day of ninth grade to be exact. On the second day my homeroom teacher, Mr. Barrett, had sent the white cards home. The ones for kids who might qualify for free lunch. I handed the card to my mother and said, "We don't need this, do we?" She said nothing.

Day three. I wiggled in my seat, palms sweaty, heart beating rapidly. I wanted to throw it away, to destroy the evidence. Instead I folded the card and dog-eared the corners to make sure no one would see as I passed it to the front. Betty was sitting right beside me swinging her crossed leg that showed off her Bass Weejuns as she absentmindedly picked lint from her Villager sweater. Betty and I had been friends since seventh grade. She was the daughter of a bank president. I always had friends who had lots more of everything than we did, but I never imagined how much more.

Four thousand dollars, that's what the card said. Not fourteen thousand but four thousand. My father had raised four daughters on less than ninety dollars a week—less than that when my sisters were young. I finally knew why all my life I'd heard, "We don't have much, but we're blessed with daughters." Four thousand dollars a year in 1963 was not much.

As tears of humiliation rimmed my eyes threatening to spill over at any moment, I wondered why I had not been treated like Mildred. Even teachers treated Mildred differently. Mildred wore tattered clothes and often smelled bad. Though Mother made all of my clothes, they were pretty and always clean. Mildred didn't have many friends. I didn't want to be her friend most of the time. She lived down the street and often came to my house to watch television. We had television. And people treated me just as they treated any of my friends.

Almost from earliest memories, I remember reading and being read to. In fact, I was as precocious then as my own daughter is today. I remember storytelling too. I remember following my mother around asking her to tell me stories. And she did. I sat on the counter as she cooked or washed dishes, and she told wonderful stories. On this day of all days, I remembered the books that lined the bookshelf in the hall outside my bedroom. *Little Women* was my favorite. I also remembered the literature anthologies with pressed flowers that had grown moldy with age. My sisters' legacy. I read these books as a kid. I read literature. And teachers treated me differently from the way they treated Mildred.

Now I don't know what grades Mildred made in school, but I always made good grades. I was a straight "A" student or "E" student; we got "E's" in grade school and then "A's" in junior high. Since I was in classes with all of my friends, I assume I was not in a low group. Though my parents never pushed me to achieve, I did because I liked school. I liked it so much that I often played school in the afternoon. Mildred was one of the few kids in my neighborhood, and she was usually willing to play most anything. I always wanted to be the teacher. Mildred was a good student, at least in my class.

But after ninth grade things changed. I didn't change and my teachers didn't either. I think they were none the wiser. But things changed all right. Oh, they didn't change with my friends either. I would never have let them know. *I did not eat free lunch!* But things definitely changed. For example, that was the last year I took algebra. The last year I took any math except general math. I never took geometry, or calculus, or trig. I took biology in tenth grade because it was required, but I never took chemistry or physics. It was general math and general science and lots of what the counselors called practical courses from then on. It was typing, shorthand, bookkeeping. It was cooking and sewing and childcare. I was being prepared for the "real world." Any idiot could figure that out.

And I didn't fight it. A teenager with a boyfriend and an interest in the social resources of schooling, I was delighted not to spend extra hours in study. I didn't think about college at the time. My parents loved me and wanted the best for me within the parameters of what they could give, but they hadn't tried to stop the endless flow of general courses either. Nothing about academic success being related to the world was discussed in my house. With little more than a grade-school education themselves, I'm sure my parents considered it an accomplishment to have gotten their daughters through high school. Given the drop-out rate of many kids from working-class homes, I'm sure of it. So I prepared for the real world gladly, not realizing until much later exactly what was happening.

Each year in March Mrs. Rayburn called students one by one to her office to help them plan the next year. In eleventh grade, when it was my turn, I wanted to know what my options might be — not for twelfth grade, but later. I quickly realized I had few. Mrs. Rayburn very candidly said, "Relax, you'll make someone a fine wife, and you can probably get a job in an office." My grades hadn't changed, but colleges don't give scholarships for general courses. Right after that she looked me straight in the eyes and said, "You can't afford college anyway." I remember my reaction. In the language of teenagers, I had been screwed! Why hadn't I seen it coming? Why would I, though? I was sixteen. My parents should have seen. But their lack of academic experience made that impossible too. And even now, I think Mrs. Rayburn thought she was acting out of the best interest of everyone involved. After all, my sisters were wives and one of them worked in an office. The other two were raising their babies. Only one of three sisters had attended any college, and she went to business school for a short while. Not that Mrs. Rayburn had helped them with their career moves; still, it was probably not an unreasonable expectation for me. How could my parents send me to college anyway? On $4,000? They didn't expect it. Why should anyone else?

That my working-class parents could not afford college, however, was not the point. Don't get me wrong, I didn't then and I don't now think there's anything wrong with being a wife and working in an office if that's what one chooses. But I hadn't chosen. By the end of eleventh grade I was angry. And even though I didn't have words for what was happening to me (like sexism and classism), I knew it must happen to other kids. It had happened to Mildred from the start. And I knew it didn't happen to kids like Betty to the same degree that it had happened to me. While she took typing and home economics, she also took all the right college-preparatory courses. She had options. High school played a role in helping that happen. Being female and poor earned me two strikes.

By twelfth grade most of my friends had already made their college plans. Oddly enough they wondered why I had made none. I wanted to go to college, but by the time I knew that, it was nearly too late. I had taken no college-preparatory courses except English, which I chose. My love for reading never died. Fortunately for me, the anger I felt and my passion for reading literature lasted, fueling a desire on my part to overcome this lack of preparation. I decided to do all I could to go to college. So I worked my way through junior college in my town, spending hours and hours in tutorials trying to catch up. The crossing was difficult, and it seemed I had traveled a thousand miles to get there. Due to a system we call tracking today, I was nearly unable to "cross the boundary" between what I might choose and what was chosen for me.

Rose (1989) suggests that many students are not invited to cross boundaries because of socioeconomic class, or race, or gender. I too have seen my experiences repeated frequently in the lives of my students. In other words, ability grouping or tracking is not always based on ability only. If someone comes from an economically less-than-privileged background, he or she tends to be treated differently in schools — as if intelligence and learning were predicated on economics. And if that someone is female, or black and female, the crossing becomes even more difficult.

Equally problematic is the fact that sometimes prejudice is subtle and may operate only at a subconscious level. This, I suspect, is even more harmful than blatant acts of racism, sexism, or classism because the prejudiced person or persons can simply feign ignorance when called upon to account for his or her actions or attitudes. Audrey, a student in one of my classes this term, told of a time when a teacher refused to let her hand in a paper early to avoid a late penalty on an assignment that was due on Rosh Hashanah, a holiday her entire family celebrated. Subtle anti-Semitism or deliberate, the outcome is harmful. But structures of inequality are not always subconscious. Often they are simply unexamined because those doing the examination feel uncomfortable about digging into such issues.

Yet children and adults alike are bombarded daily in nearly every form of media with inappropriate treatment of women and minorities.

People are stereotyped on the basis of gender, race, ethnicity, age, class, physical difference, and sexual orientation. Such negative representations of groups of people, as if everyone in those groups were the same, is a social phenomenon. Yet, we are ever so frequently reminded that prejudices are sanctioned repeatedly in classrooms, in textbooks, in literature, in the media, and so forth.

One possibility for breaking down the barriers of cultural stereotypes is that schools take a more active role in the development of moral sensibilities. Understanding the ways in which students define themselves and others is a step toward such development. Helping young people develop in fair-minded ways, considering equity in all situations, is another important part of that development.

But Why the Schools?

Teachers interested in how students learn to consider and appreciate other viable perspectives, how their value systems develop, and how they see themselves in relation to others will recognize the importance in teaching matters of equity. Beginning this process early, perhaps as early as fifth grade, may help students become sensitive to institutionalized roles for women and minorities (roles like mother, secretary, nurse, even teacher are traditionally considered woman's work) by the time they are old enough to begin considering alternative situations (Abrams, 1981).

Because schools are seen by parents and children alike as sanctioning certain attitudes, behaviors, and lifestyles, it seems crucial that schools take an active role in helping young people develop moral sensibilities with respect to issues of class, race, and gender. If schools play a role in developing such sensibilities, there is greater likelihood that students will question and even condemn inappropriate treatment of women and minorities both in curricular materials and in society at large.

A course or unit on cultural stereotypes celebrates diversity by providing experiences that help students become aware of the pervasiveness of sexism, racism, homophobia, ablebodiedness, and stereotypes aimed at Native Americans and international cultures. For example, prejudice against Jewish and Arab people is especially prevalent within our society at this particular moment in history. Fortunately, curricular materials are already beginning to reflect the need to deal with equity issues.

Many English departments are now including significant works by women and minority authors. Teachers and curriculum specialists are recognizing that some traditional textbooks and literary texts fall short of accurately presenting women's and minorities' contributions to literature, history, and culture. Books for children and young adults also offer an exciting possibility for teaching about the prevalence of stereotypes within our society. Middle and high school students as well as college students can learn a lot about the mythological origins of sexism, racism, and classism through examination of fairy tales and nursery rhymes.

Likewise, children's literature about African-American experience can help clarify how racial stereotyping takes place. It's often the case that such books present a selective or slanted version of black history, which contributes to racist attitudes. For example, in spite of winning the coveted Newbery Award in 1970, *Sounder* (1969), written by William H. Armstrong, is full of racist overtones and is not a true rendering of black history. Or, as Tom Feelings, a black artist and critic, suggests, if true as told by the story teller, then it is true only to the extent that a black man or woman would be able to tell the truth to his or her oppressor while under oppression. Albert Schwartz (1972) quotes Feelings and other critics in his appraisal of *Sounder* as a mostly white tale. None of the characters in this book has a name except the dog, Sounder. Sounder's family lives in complete isolation. They have no relationships with anyone except a Black minister, and the Bible stories the mother tells are all from a white fundamentalist perspective. When I use this book in a study of racist stereotyping, students have little difficulty seeing racist overtones in the story. However, without opportunity for discussion, many award-winning books like *Sounder* often get an automatic seal of approval from many teachers, parents, and especially children. Since this book provides no positive role model for black readers, *Sounder* would likely perpetuate a stereotype of "worthlessness," particularly among white readers. Moreover, "the black experience" is told in this book and in others as if there were *one* experience among African-American peoples.

Ann Trousdale (1990) provides a rich description of *Sounder* and other prize-winning books that are frequently read and praised by teachers and children alike but that misrepresent or present a selective version of African-American life. Moreover, she juxtaposes these books with several other award-winning titles that seem to present a less stereotyped image of black people. *Roll of Thunder, Hear My Cry* (1976) by Mildred Taylor is an excellent example of such a book.

Teachers can cover many of the important topics that deal with stereotypes in books for children and young adults. The following topics are important when I teach a course on women and minorities: women on the frontier, gender constructions, sexual identities, appearance and capability, native North Americans, African-American experiences, international cultures, anti-Semitism and other religious and geographic prejudices.

Recent emphasis on the study of stereotyping has produced a variety of annotated book lists aimed at helping middle and high school students explore issues of class, gender, ethnicity, and so forth. For example, *English Journal* has at least two book lists I've used regularly for selecting books to teach about stereotypes (Booksearch, 1989; Wilson, 1984). Another rich source of information on books about the Jewish Holocaust has been collected by Joan F. Kaywell (1989).

Approaches to Teaching About Cultural Stereotypes

Since we are important models for students, it is necessary in all ways that our classrooms reflect our positions on issues of equity. Therefore, everything from bulletin-board displays (e.g., collection of newspaper clippings showing women participating in a variety of sports or careers and clippings of minorities involved in a variety of leadership and other important roles) to our behavior during class discussions needs to reflect equitable attitudes and practices (Abrams, 1981). For example, I have discovered that discussion occurs more equitably within smaller groups. Though I sit with my students in a circle during whole-class discussion, I still create a "back of the room." That is, students sitting closest to me on either side participate the most. Those farther away may say nothing. Furthermore, my students expect me to help them feel comfortable sharing their concerns and beliefs about sensitive materials. Since personal-experience stories are often told in small-group discussions, it is useful to have a set of guidelines for discussion. When students know that we respect and value their contributions, they will be more likely to listen to other voices thoughtfully and participate in group sharing more frequently. Students want us to make classroom participation as safe and nonthreatening as possible. Following are some guidelines I use:

- NO HUNTING—that is, no "cheap shots" or "put-downs" to anyone for what he or she is saying for any reason.

- Everyone has something important to say and should be given a chance to say it—only one person can be heard at a time, so please, no interruptions.
- Listen carefully when someone is speaking.
- Consider everyone's contribution equally important.

Dealing with sensitive materials

With respect to sensitive issues, it is extremely important that we allow students to learn from the literature and/or other media rather than from us. For example, a book or story selection that blatantly, exposes stereotypes will speak for itself. *Sounder* is an excellent example of how the literature we choose can address certain issues without our deliberately focusing upon them.

Selecting a book that illumines class, race, and gender formulations and one capable of speaking for itself tends to relieve the defensiveness with which some students react to such material. Because students can respond to the text and not to something we teach about that text, sensitive materials can be dealt with more easily and without creating a threatening situation for some students. On the other hand, this course of action requires that we feel secure about not being totally in control of the discussion. As an approach it tends to demystify the traditional teacher-as-expert image. As we break with the lecture model of teaching or the teacher-directed question-and-answer-session model, it becomes natural to encourage student-led questioning and discussing of socio-cultural tensions around stereotyped characters.

As this process unfolds, students become less inhibited and are eager to relate characters and situations to events in their own lives. When my students read books and view other materials with stereotyped characters, they tell stories relating events and attitudes from their reading to personal experiences. Storytelling, then, becomes a powerful model for discovering who we are and how we stand in relation to others. As we share stories, almost everyone remembers either being mistreated themselves at some time or other or knowing someone who has been mistreated on the basis of prejudice. Finally, students begin to understand that the purpose of studying this and other literature is not for uncovering "one correct" meaning in the text but for exploring texts and making meanings or interpretations based on their own experience (Rosenblatt, 1976/1938).

Yet the study of stereotypes need not be limited to books. While examining stereotypes in books allows us a glimpse at how literature not only influences but perpetuates certain images of women and minorities, it is probably equally necessary to look at local and media influences in order to develop a thorough understanding. Sometimes students need to look beyond their own experience to the lives of family, friends, and other members of the community to study prejudice created by or perpetuated in the stereotyping of certain groups. For example, I have students research the cultural stereotyping in their own classes and on campus as a whole. They keep a log of each instance of someone being referred to in a derogatory manner if the remark stereotyped that person. Students particularly report hearing "fag" and "lesbo." Younger students might note hearing "sissy" or "tomboy" or "queer" or "fatso" and so forth. Students discuss what images those names create. What is implied in a name? How do such names affect their own self-image? How does name-calling make one feel about the person or persons to whom the name is addressed? They also note any mistreatment by themselves or other students of people of color, people who are handicapped or who have physical limitations, like size, for example. They especially note how stereotyped people are treated by teachers.

Though such an assessment focuses the student outward, still it requires looking closely at experiences. What students need to center upon in examining stereotypes is how typecasting regards individuals in generalized ways (which tends also to be negative) rather than recognizing their uniqueness and human potential.

Studying Stereotypes in Popular Culture

Although much is made of studying stereotypes in literature, little attention is paid to forms of stereotyping in popular culture, in music, television, advertising, and movies. Given the amount of time young people currently spend on media-related activities, this may be one of our most valuable options for showing students the degree to which they are being enculturated, or even indoctrinated through cultural patterns reflected in popular culture. For example, students tell me that television and music have a way of desensitizing them to behaviors and attitudes so that what might be seen as inappropriate on first glance is no longer noticed after much viewing and listening. In any case, asking students to evaluate strengths and weaknesses in literature and popular culture based upon the extent to which such portrayal influences women's and minorities' status in society may help them to consider more equitable roles for women (as well as men) and minorities.

A Projects Approach to Studying Cultural Stereotypes

Activities designed to enhance the study of cultural stereotypes should get students closer to those personal experiences that influence and perpetuate their own images of women and minorities. If we recognize the amount of attention given to music, movies, television, advertising, even shopping, then it seems essential that we include these areas in a study of stereotyping. In-depth examination with primary data and personal engagement may be our best hope of reversing students' negative images of themselves and others (Abrams, 1981).

The most important thing about projects in any learning environment is that they provide students with options. There need to be options that include working individually and with others collaboratively. All invitations to study more about the roles of women and minorities will no doubt raise students' awareness of the problems cultural stereotyping can cause in our society. The following ideas, some of which were suggested by teachers I've worked with, might be a place to begin:

1. Images that suggest sex-role identities (I suggest whole-class brainstorming and discussion for this activity):
   A. Consider the roles of men and women commonly found on magazine covers, in advertising, in movies and television (also in books). Generate a list of attributes suggested by these images. What roles are given to males only? to females only? What emotions are expressed only by males? by females? Is there a range of family groupings—e.g., single mother, single father, interracially mixed families?
   B. Try to remember the last time you saw a toy in a department store or a commercial for one on television. Make a list of toys that are marketed specifically for boys, specifically for girls. Make a list of toys that are marketed for either sex. Which ones are most popular? Do a small survey of toy stores to discover which ones sell the most.
   C. Think about the tools, machines, and equipment in your home. What tools are located where in your house? Who

is associated with using those tools? For example, who uses kitchen tools (coffee pot or coffee maker, cooking pans, knives, mixer, blender, etc.) most in your house? Who uses the lawnmower? What images are associated with using various tools?

D. What images are associated with various occupations? Examine television or movies to see how frequently certain jobs are designated by gender (or examine your own textbooks or library books). Brainstorm a list of jobs that you know only males or only females work in. Why do you suppose those jobs are filled specifically by males or females? What job do you wish to have in the future? Have images of gender-specific career choices affected your decisions thus far? Create your own list of nongender-specific jobs.

E. What's in a title? Think about professional or even nonprofessional titles. Look at the language of those titles (e.g., house*wife*, fire*man*, etc.). What images do those titles suggest? Make a list of sexist titles, and then create their nonsexist equivalents.

Similar versions of these and other projects have been developed and field-tested by the Curriculum Office of the School District of Philadelphia to emphasize educational equity (Abrams, 1981). Projects 1A through 1E are designed to help students understand how our culture socializes us into gendered roles. But gendered roles are by no means the only ones subject to cultural stereotyping. Other project opportunities focus equally on ethnicity or class or stereotypes of physical appearance:

2. Examine cultural stereotypes in, at least, five television programs (including cartoons), movies, commercials or ads, and so forth (or three books including picture books for children). Note the situations in which each observed instance of stereotyping occurs. Write about the roles given people of color, people from various ethnic groups, handicapped peoples, and so forth. In your paper, discuss the ways in which people who are fat or who have various physical limitations are portrayed. In other words, are the main characters usually ablebodied and beautiful? Does this suggest what our society values? Do you see much cultural variation? Talk about this. For example, how are Native Americans portrayed? How are people from

various socioeconomic classes portrayed? What family groupings do you see? Are there interracial families in your sample?

3. Listen to popular music. What images do certain lyrics create? Do they create specific images of males and females or people of color? Keep a log for one week.

4. Assess the stereotyping in newspaper cartoons. Cut out as many examples as you can find and create a class collage. You may wish to create your own cartoons that are free of cultural stereotypes.

5. Watch the news or read a newspaper. Who is represented as powerful in our society? Do men and women of every race and nationality find role models in positions of leadership and authority? Write a journal entry reporting your findings over a period of a week.

6. Read the sports section of a newspaper. Count the number of articles about male athletes versus female athletes. How are black males portrayed in relation to white males? Clip articles that show women participating in nonstereotypical sports. Do the same for men. Make a bulletin board display for your class.

7. Write a story using nonsexist language and creating characters who are nonstereotypical in terms of class, race, physical abilities and limitations, and so forth. Think about the ingredients of such a story. What kinds of things do your female characters do? How do they dress? What do they talk about? What about the males? What emotions are expressed by each? What family groupings are in your story? What roles do people of various ethnic backgrounds play in your story?

8. Create your own project that in some way helps you further understand and fight cultural stereotypes. If resources permit, present such initiatives in the form of video or in other visual ways. Discuss the differences, if any, in visual images and images derived from print.

The more often we allow students to make conscious choices with respect to projects, the more we will have a chance to assess the outcomes of a study of this nature because their choices and the levels of achievement in those choices will vary according to degree of awareness and understanding.

Each activity or mini-research project asks students to relate the primary data they collect to situations from personal experience.

Questions invite values clarification as they help students confront fears and assess strengths. Additionally, activities require students to consider their own sources of strength in handling a variety of situations, even threatening ones. Such inventory-taking tends to expand students' self-images. Yet, perhaps of equal importance, studying cultural stereotypes shows us how we are continually shaping and being shaped, albeit sometimes subtly, by other members of society.

Teachers need to be aware of the serious difference between a biased or even adequate English curriculum and one that stresses the contributions of all members of society. Both curricula can teach language arts, but only one that includes and credits women and minorities can encourage *all* students to believe in themselves and their potential. Teachers committed to educational equity have the opportunity to make a significant difference in how young people view themselves and their world.

REFERENCES

Abrams, E. (1981). *A curriculum guide to women's studies for middle school, grades 5–9.* New York: The Feminist Press.

Armstrong, W. H. (1969). *Sounder.* New York: Harper & Row.

Booksearch. (September 1989). Breaking down cultural stereotypes. *English Journal,* 88–90.

Kaywell, J. F. (November 1989). *Young adult literature as a complement to the classics.* Paper presented at the National Council of Teachers of English Fall Conference, Baltimore, MD.

McCann, D., and Woodard, G. (Eds.), *The Black American in books for children.* Metuchen, NJ: The Scarecrow Press.

Rose, M. (1989). *Lives on the boundary.* New York: Penguin.

Rosenblatt, L. M. (1976/1938). *Literature as exploration.* New York: The Modern Language Association of America.

Schwartz, A. V. (1972). *Sounder:* A black or white tale? In D. McCann and G. Woodard (Eds.), *The Black American in books for children.* Metuchen, NJ: The Scarecrow Press.

Taylor, M. D. (1976). *Roll of thunder, hear my cry.* New York: Bantam Books.

Trousdale, A. M. (1990). A submission theology for black Americans: Religion and social action in prize winning children's books about the black experience in America. *Research in the Teaching of English 24*(2), 117–140.

Wilson, D. E. (November 1984). The open library: YA books for gay teens. *English Journal,* 60–63.

ADDITIONAL READINGS FOR TEACHERS

Bulletin. Council on Interracial Books for Children, 1841 Broadway, New York, NY 10023.

Christian-Smith, L. (1988). Romancing the girl: Adolescent romance novels and the construction of femininity. In L. Roman, L. Christian-Smith, and E. Ellsworth (Eds.), *Becoming feminine: The politics of popular culture*. New York: The Falmer Press.

Council on Interracial Books for Children. (1976). *Human and anti-human values in children's books*. New York: Racism and Sexism Resource Center.

Dixon, B. (1977). *Catching them young: Political ideas in children's fiction*. London: Pluto Press.

Frazier, N., and Sadker, M. (1973). *Sexism in school and society*. New York: Harper and Row.

Gitlin, T. (Ed.). (1986). *Watching television: A Pantheon guide to popular culture*. New York: Pantheon Books.

Gitlin, T. (1983). *Inside prime time*. New York: Pantheon Books.

Guttentag, M., and Bray, H. (1976). *Undoing sex stereotypes*. New York: McGraw-Hill.

Haller, E. (1977). *New perspectives: A bibliography of racial, ethnic, and feminist resources*. Bureau of Curriculum Services, Pennsylvania Department of Education, P.O. Box 911, Harrisburg, PA 17126.

Klein, G. (1985). *Reading into racism: Bias in children's literature and learning materials*. London: Routledge and Kegan Paul.

Racism and Sexism Resource Center for Educators. (1979). *Winning "Justice for all."* New York: Racism and Sexism Resource Center. A curriculum unit for grades five and six on sexism and racism may be ordered from the Council on Interracial Books for Children, 1841 Broadway, New York, NY 10023.

Sims, R. (1982). *Shadow and substance: Afro-American experience in contemporary children's books*. Urbana, IL: National Council of Teachers of English.

Taxel, J. (1978–1979). Justice and cultural conflict: Racism, sexism, and instructional materials. *Interchange* 9(1), 56–84.

Walkerdine, V. (1985). On the regulation of speaking and silence: Subjectivity, class, and gender in contemporary schooling. In C. Steedman, C. Urwin, V. Walkerdine (Eds.), *Language, Gender, and Childhood*. London: Routledge and Kegan Paul.

Weitzman, L. (1973). Sex-role socialization in picture books. *American Journal of Sociology* 77(6), 1125–1150.

Whalen-Levitt, P. (1980). Literature and child readers. *Children's Literature Association Quarterly* 4(4), 9–13.

Autobiography and Authority in the Study of Composition and Literature

*David Schaafsma and
Michael Smith*
University of Wisconsin — Madison

*I*n the last decade a chorus of voices has called for student empowerment. Research and theory on both the composing process and response to literature have placed the spotlight on students as active meaning makers and have done much to dispel the image of students as passive recipients of knowledge. We celebrate this fundamental change in our professions, but we do so with some degree of caution. We believe that truly empowering students means more than giving them the *opportunity* to write and to read, a conception that informs much instruction. Rather we believe that it means helping them develop *authority* in their reading and writing. To us this means both helping students develop their textual power and increasing their willingness to use it. Scholes (1985) shares our concern when he explains his vision of a teacher's task:

> Reading and writing are complementary acts that remain unfinished until they are completed by their reciprocals. ... [M]y writing is unfinished until it is read by others ... whose responses may become

known to me, engendering new textualities. We have an endless web here, of growth, and change, and interaction, learning, and forgetting, dialogue and dialectic. Our task as teachers is to introduce students to this web, to make it real and visible for them, insofar as we can, and to encourage them to cast their own strands of thought and text into this network so that they will feel its power and understand how to use it and how to protect themselves from its abuses. (pp. 20–21)

We have found that having students tell their own stories is an exciting and effective way of helping them develop their textual power and encouraging them to employ it.

Many teachers overlook autobiographical stories as a primitive form, something "every student can do," something students need to outgrow or move "beyond" for the learning they will have to do in schools. Stories may be entertaining, these teachers might say, and the process of storytelling may be personally useful to individual storytellers, but the story form would seem to have questionable use in the serious accumulation of knowledge that must take place in school.

Stories, grounded as they are in students' lives and concerns, are one very important means students have for making sense of their worlds. As psychologist Jerome Bruner says, stories are one "way of exploring possible worlds out of the context of immediate need" (1986, p. 123). This view of stories is consistent with Maxine Greene's notion of what she calls "emancipatory education" as "a process of discovery and recovery in response to worthwhile questions rising out of conscious life in concrete situations" (1978, p. 44).

Autobiography in the Composition Classroom

Because Dora consistently performs poorly on various school measures, and partly because she is feisty and tough and gets in occasional fights, she has for years generally been assigned to the "Reading Lab" at her school. When she was in second and third grades, then reading specialist Debi worked with her and helped her learn to read and write better. She was also later a student in Debi's fifth-grade class, and through it Debi recruited her for The Dewey Center Community Writing Project (a Detroit inner-city summer writing program) during which the following story was written.

961–BABY

Dora S.

Lynn was having a baby. As she get out of the car at the hospital, she looked like she had a pillow under her coat. She said to Don, "I can't take it any more, O.K."

Don didn't answer.

"I knew it was about to come," said Lynn.

"How are you doing," Don asked.

"Just fine . . . Ohhhhh."

Lynn was 23 and had four kids and one on the way. She dropped out of high school at the age of 15. When she was 16, she got pregnant. Her mom put her out when she found out that she dropped out of school. Her mom was very sad that she had put out her only child.

"Right on time, honey."

"You know I can't take care of all these children."

"You only have four, and one on the way," Don said.

Lynn walked into emergency and Don left. On the way home, Don didn't think about what Lynn said.

Three days later Lynn came home with a new baby. Lynn walked in the bedroom, and found Don's clothes were gone.

Now she had five children. It was very hard to get things done around the house. The seven-year-old wouldn't obey her and wouldn't help her. The two-year-old threw paper and milk. The baby would holler. The four- and five-year-olds were always fighting.

Lynn felt exhausted. She would go outside and get a stick and hit the kids. Then she felt bad. She didn't want to hit her children.

She looked in the newspaper and saw an ad that said, "If you can't take care of your kids, call us, and we will help you; 961–BABY. So she called. Mrs. Bell answered the phone, "Hello, how may we help you?"

"I need help with my children."

"I can help you but you have to promise to get your G.E.D., OK?"

"I'll try."

Mrs. Bell then asked, "You have to help us, too. What do you know how to do?"

Lynn said, "Nothing."

"Can you wash clothes? Can you cook? Can you clean?"

"Yes," said Lynn.

Mrs. Bell found day care for Lynn's kids, so Lynn could go to school in the morning. The teacher at the day care helped Lynn and the children learned to cooperate. The kids started to obey and help. Lynn got the rest that she needed.

Lynn called her mother and told her mother what she was doing. Lynn's mother helped her with the kids, too.

Then two years later, Lynn came to Mrs. Bell and said, "I made it."

(The Dewey Center Community Writing Project, 1989, pp. 32–33)

The summer writing program teachers' initial impression of Dora in the program was generally a negative one. One teacher's notes for the first day of the program are sketchy, but useful in indicating the general feeling about her. He wrote, "Dora—Hyper kid, bossy, didn't do much today." But another teacher saw Dora's notes on a first-day group interview with longtime inner-city resident Rose Bell, and documented how those notes on the stories of Ms. Bell took shape through peer comments and her own thoughtful revision.

"961—BABY" is a "fictional" story, but it is also in many ways an autobiographical one, connected to Dora's own life. The impetus for the story came from an interview with Ms. Rose Bell, whose words are here in Dora's text, but it is also important to know that some of Dora's middle school friends had dropped out of school because they had become pregnant. In addition to that, Dora's mother is, like Lynn, a single parent raising Dora and her brothers, sisters, and cousins with little help. The stories that Ms. Bell told helped Dora think of her own and her close friends' life stories. As Dora explained to David one day,

> DORA: She had a group of old people helping out teenagers and their babies, who can't feed them and stuff like that, and she brought it up and we asked her about it and she told us that she had a number, which was 961—BABY, and I thought about writing a story about it, and I made a story up.
>
> DAVID: Uh-huh. How did you think of that story?
>
> DORA: Because when she said she helped little kids and their babies, I thought about that it should be nice to write a story about little kids and their babies.

There are other voices in Dora's story, too. Dora's writing developed as a result of our working closely and intensively with her in small group workshops and in conferences, by helping her revise on a computer, by helping her make meaning for herself about things she felt were most important to write about, by emphasizing her strengths and not her apparent deficiencies as an evolving maker of meaning for herself. Though she can proudly claim ownership of the final product, during the process she spoke to teachers and peers in daily writing workshops and conferences. She shared the story in process with family and friends. In all of the responses to her writing those of us who were her readers wanted to reinforce her enthusiasm for writing and learning and validate her experiences in her community. Dora's story is one that builds with experience, not neatly, not without struggle, but piece by piece with the careful attention of teachers and peers and family members. It is their voices that join her own and Ms. Bell's voices in "961–BABY." When she was done with the story we asked her why she had written it, and she said:

> DORA: There's a lot of kids I know in the Projects who have babies, and they don't know what to do. They dropped out of high school and they had them, and then they stay with their mother a couple of years, and they go back to high school and they miss their friends. . . . And it's like friends don't want to talk to them at all, because they have a baby and stuff like that.
>
> DAVID: So that's why you wrote the story?
>
> DORA: I don't know. I liked what Ms. Bell had to say and what she's doing for young teenaged mothers. A couple of friends of mine went to her and they are doing real well. I don't know. Maybe if they read my story, they might have some hope that they can make it, too.

Autobiography and Authority

Dora's "961–BABY" exhibits a certain kind of rhetorical authority. She demonstrates a kind of power as storyteller that surprised many who were her teachers: a growing facility for dialogue, detail, metaphor. She illustrates some qualities we would hope all writers would have, such as making use of multiple sources, integrating her own experience with the experience of others. She shows evidence of developing control as a writer. For a student having just completed fifth grade, and especially for one who has primarily been assigned to "remedial" classes (where students typically don't get to write very much), "961–BABY" is a remarkable story. It is pretty compelling evidence that autobiographical writing can be a way to develop rhetorical skills.

In addition to the rhetorical strengths that her story exhibits, the kind of knowledge Dora seems to have created bears certain similarities to the "personal" knowledge that chemist Michael Polanyi describes (1962), a way of knowing that is invested with intentionality, passionate and experiential. Polanyi's emphasis on the autonomy and commitment of the individual knower is consistent with the way many write about narrative, as a primarily "personal," or individual, act or process. Many narrative theorists emphasize the psychological aspects of the process of storytelling. For instance, Barbara Hardy puts an emphasis on cognitive functions when she identifies narrative as a "primary act of mind" (1968, p. 73). Teacher Betty Rosen sees stories as "a way of dealing with matters of deep concern in people's lives" (1988, p. 17), emphasizing the "therapeutic" value of stories. As with journal writing, it may be "good" for you to talk through your problems and difficult experiences, and make sense of them. Others emphasize the importance of the use of the imagination, the uses of metaphor and fantasy in storytelling, or the way it can help students develop "authentic voice." As Gordon Wells puts it, "The education of the whole person, which is the declared aim of probably every school system, can only be achieved if there are opportunities to explore feelings and values in specific real or imagined situations as well as lessons devoted to the considerations of general principles" (1986, p. 203). For Wells, these opportunities primarily include engagement in storytelling, as readers and writers of stories.

Many composition theorists, such as Ken Macrorie, champion the story for similar reasons. Viewing much student writing as stilted and artificial "Engfish," Macrorie (1970) sees stories as writing based in personal experience for readers and writers, to be valued particularly for their demonstration of "voice." Voice in this tradition is often closely related to the emotions, presumably "repressed" in most academic writing. We could usefully describe Dora's story in terms of its "voice," perhaps, or speculate on how she works out certain personal concerns through her autobiographical writing. We might even discuss with her, as we did, why she wrote in the story form at all, and come to an understanding of her uses of narrative. At any rate, various psychological considerations regarding the study of narrative writing can certainly be useful.

As important as the rhetorical and "psychological" benefits of telling stories might be, there are still more important considerations involved when we ask our students to write autobiographical stories in our classrooms. The nature of narrative is such that in stories multiple voices are preserved, multiple perspectives. These voices point to the social nature of stories. The voices present in Dora's text, as we've pointed out, are the voices of the people she has interviewed, the voices of her peer, teacher, and family readers and writers, the voices of characters in other texts she has read, interacting with her own emerging voices. Dora's story can be seen as an artistically organized means for bringing different voices in contact with one another, testing them against one another. The languages of the others whom we learn from/with are present in each instance of our language use, in all of our talk and writing with one another, but they are voices, often consciously suppressed in other forms, that are emphasized in the social exploration that is narrative. If we can come to see the fundamentally social character of language and learning, and recognize the ways in which narrative highlights the social nature of language, then we can begin to appreciate the possibilities for autobiographical story writing in the process of learning about the world and making sense of experience.

Henry Louis Gates, talking about the cultural value of storytelling, says:

> The stories that we tell ourselves and our children function to order our world, serving to create both a foundation upon which each of us constructs our sense of reality and a filter through which we process each event that confronts us every day. The values that we cherish and wish to preserve, the behavior that we wish to censure, the fears and dread that we can barely confess in ordinary language, the aspirations and goals that we most dearly prize—all of these things are encoded in the stories that, in effect, we live by and through. (1989, p. 17)

Dora's story helps her to "order her world"; it demonstrates the power of autobiographical writing in the classroom, and demonstrates as well a kind of authority, developed with teachers and peers, that attests to the personal and cultural value of storytelling.

Patti Stock's study of Susan, in "The Dialogic Curriculum: Students and Teachers Researching Together," is helpful in understanding how stories about one's world might serve learning in schools. Of Susan's writing Stock writes:

> In her composition, Susan combines elements from her lived world and her studies; she does not change their identities, but retains them, in clarified form. In her act of composition, Susan's past experiences and her studies each come to mean something different in the light of one another. In this sense, each is transformed, becomes something else, existing at a new level of complexity. Susan, I would argue, becomes someone else, someone able to live in the world she can imagine, the world she composes . . . (1991, p. 27)

Dora, too, composes texts, and through "961—BABY" composes a self and a world. Her past experiences and her present study are transformed, and in that transformation she is transformed, too. That transformation for Dora takes place through storytelling: through the stories of the people she has interviewed, including Rose Bell, through the stories of her peer, teacher, and family readers and writers who tell her own story back to her and tell their own stories to her, through the voices of characters in other texts she has read, interacting with her own emerging voices.

Students such as Dora can help us understand the ways in which the social acts of story making create both selves and culture. In this framework, autobiographical writing functions in part as a means of exploration, an investigation of possibilities. But this exploration, to be truly empowering, must take place in a community where members negotiate meanings together, and in a community that supports that exploration and helps students in developing authority. Stories, as one important potentially empowering form of writing, are more than just tools for individual imagination and self-discovery. As Jerome Bruner says, narrative provides a "map of possible roles and possible worlds in which action, thought, and self-definition are permissible (or desirable)" (1986, p. 66).

Students like Dora, writing stories, explore both personal "roles" and cultural "possible worlds" through the writing of autobiographical stories. Dora demonstrates the kind of necessary, conscious exploration that Bruner and Greene talk about as she, with others, investigates possible roles and possible worlds for herself through her story. She is, with the help of her peers and teachers and the person she interviewed, creating knowledge for her own purposes, shaping (and being shaped by) stories as her way of knowing, her way of learning.

Autobiographical Writing in the Study of Literature

Just as students must exercise authority if they are to be effective writers, so too must they exercise authority when they read literature. It is especially crucial that students have the authority to apply their life experiences, for as literary theory, reading research, and research in response to literature have demonstrated, such application is crucial if readers are to have meaningful transactions with texts.

Unfortunately, we have found that students often do not make effective use of their personal experience when they read, as examples of students' think-aloud protocol responses to John Collier's story "The Chaser" indicate. In "The Chaser" a young man seeks to buy a love potion from a mysterious old man who has a number of extraordinary potions, including a poison "quite imperceptible to any known method of autopsy" for which he charges $5,000 a teaspoon. Although the young man is horrified by the poison, he is delighted when the old man tells him that he charges but a dollar for the love potion, a potion that would make him the sole focus of his lover's life. The young man leaves with the potion and says goodbye to the old man. "Au revoir," the old man replies. The story turns on the conflict between the young man's naive view of love and the old man's cynicism. Readers are invited to understand that the old man will indeed see the young man again after he tires of his love and comes back for the other potion.

To investigate student's responses we asked them to verbalize everything they thought of as they read, the technique that we feel comes closest to capturing their actual mental activity (cf. Dias, 1987). Here's how Jerry, a ninth-grader, responded as he read the first paragraph of the story (Jerry's remarks are in italics):

> Alan Austen, as a nervous kitten, *um, num, Alan Austin is like a Kitten right now, I'm thinking*, went up a, up, certain dark and creaky stairs in the neighborhood of Pell Street, and peered about for a long time on the dim landing before he found the name he had written obscurely on one of the doors. *Now I'm thinking that, he's like, jumping . . . t, on the house or something, um. . . .*

Throughout his reading, Jerry was entirely bound by the text. He is either unable to link his lived experience to his reading or, what is more likely, he doesn't realize that it is the reader's role to make those links. Elizabeth makes personal associations with the text, but she does so almost at random:

> Alan Austen, as nervous as a kitten, went up a certain dark and creaky stairs in the neighborhood of Pell Street, and peered about for a long time on the dim landing before he found the name he wanted written obscurely on one of the doors. *Reminds me of, we have stairs in our house that go down to our cellar that are really . . . creaky!*
>
> *Um*, he pushed open this door, as he had been told to, and found himself in a tiny room, which contained no furniture but a plain kitchen table, a rocking chair, and an ordinary chair. *Reminds me of something I saw on TV last night.* On one of the dirty, buff-colored walls were a couple of shelves, containing in all perhaps . . . a dozen bottles and jars. *The shelves remind me of, trying to remember the word "shelves" in Spanish!*

Elizabeth apparently is not able to control the connections she makes or to use them to enrich her reading. Even students who make relevant connections often fail to use them to inform their reading. For example, Eavenson (1988) explains that one of the students in her study had what seems to be the crucial insight when the old man explains that the potion would make the young man's love terribly jealous and eternally vigilant. He exclaims: "Sounds like your ma! I'd hate to have a ma again when you're older." Yet by the end of the story he says, "I wish I knew somebody like that. I'd buy them phials [of love potion] and sell them for big money," apparently giving up the insight that he made. Perhaps this reader didn't have the confidence to recognize that he had a superior understanding to that of the character in the story and as a consequence, he gave up this understanding.

In our work with a number of teachers we have found that having students write about relevant autobiographical experiences before they read helps overcome these problems. To use autobiographical writing before reading, teachers identify an issue that is central to a text and ask students to write about personal experiences they have had that relate to that issue before they read. The key to writing effective prompts is to identify issues with which students will have had some experiences but ones that might not be readily evoked by the text. Effective prompts should be open-ended, cuing neither an appropriate written response to nor an interpretation of the story.

Contrast the above students with Kathy, who responds as Elizabeth and Jerry did to "The Chaser," only after having written about related autobiographical experiences. Kathy reads the entire story with no comment, then responds:

> Ooh. I like it. I do. God, I don't know if I could live my life with having someone that possessive of me. I don't think I would ever want that, not even for a dollar. That's just too bizarre. To have someone love me, yes, I can understand. But not jealous, not worried and not terrified, and not ... I want to say, I guess, almost slavish. No, I would not want that in a relationship.

Both Elizabeth and Kathy are "good" readers, and both seem to have made connections between their personal lives and the story in question. However, only Kathy's connections seem to enhance her understanding of the story and of her life. Kathy's statements demonstrate that she has reflected on the significance of her experience and that her reflections have contributed to both her understanding and her enjoyment of the story.

Simply asking students to write about their lives as preparation for reading vests them an authority they may otherwise not feel and demonstrates to them a teacher's belief in the importance of students' connecting their lives to the literature they read. In addition, by writing about their experiences students must reconsider them. This increases the likelihood that they will be able to reconstruct them from memory.

Autobiographical writing before reading appears to have positive effects on both students' understanding of and attitude toward literature. Perhaps most compellingly, autobiographical writing appears to increase students' personal investment in the study of literature, the willingness to become personally involved while interacting with subject matter and classmates. In the first place, students appear to like stories better when they write about relevant autobiographical experience before they read. In two studies, two classes of each of two teachers read and discussed two stories, one for which they had written about relevant autobiographical experience before they read and the other for which they did no writing. The story for which they did the writing changed by class. When asked which story they preferred, students were unanimous in selecting the story for which they had done the writing. And they couldn't understand how their fellow students could have selected the other story. Further, while the students who had not written before reading engaged in comparatively empty and boring discussions, the students who had written before reading engaged in more fast-paced, thoughtful give-and-take (Hamann, Schultz, Smith, and White, 1990; Smith and White in press). Finally, as White's (1990) study strongly suggests, autobiographical writing before reading may enhance younger adolescents' understanding of literary characters by helping them to move beyond surface descriptions and to focus more on abstract character traits.

Conclusion

The Holmes Report on education makes it clear what perspective drives most schooling: "Far too many teachers give out directions, busywork, and fact-fact-fact lectures in ways that keep students intellectually passive, if not actually deepening their disregard for learning and schooling" (1986, p. 7). Henry Giroux sees schools similarly, as primarily concerned with "breaking down knowledge into discrete parts, standardized for easier management consumption, and measured through predefined forms of assessment" (1988, p. 124). Teachers are often what Michel Foucault might call the "arbiters of properness" in schools, the "keepers of the gate," rather than the kind of teachers Jay Robinson and Patti Stock describe: ". . . quite deliberately trying to fashion in the classroom an inhabitable world for students, one in which they might safely raise such voices as they have to make meanings for themselves and others, voices that will be valued for such agency as they can manage" (1990, p. 312).

If we can agree that students' stories might have fundamental value in learning, why do we limit access to this way of knowing for students? As Valerie Polakow says, "Stories are where we must begin. . . . Stories are the clues which will lead us to new ways of knowing" (1985, p. 833), ways of knowing which are social, experiential, passionate, and grounded in the life worlds of our student writers. Dora's stories certainly demonstrate the value of narrative knowing in the learning they do about their lives.

We need to reconsider the value of storytelling and story writing in the learning process, especially if we are to consider how schools might speak to and with our students, especially those who feel bored, powerless, disenfranchised, those who are angry, even violent. Stories are a way to learn in school, and one possible avenue for the culture of the community, the students' various home communities, and students' ways of knowing, to intersect with the culture of schools.

Maxine Greene suggests: schools should provide "occasions for individuals to articulate the themes of their own existence" (1978, p. 18). One important way they can do this is through stories they share with one another and teachers and communities, stories shared in both reading and writing.

REFERENCES

Bruner, J. (1986). *Actual minds, possible worlds.* Cambridge: Harvard University Press.

Dias, D. (1987). Making sense of poetry: Patterns in the process. Ottawa: Canadian Council of Teachers of English.

Eavenson, R. (1988). "A comparison of the processes of good and poor high school readers while reading a short story." Unpublished manuscript.

Foucault, M. (1979). Interview with Lucette Finas. In *Michel Foucault: power, truth, strategy.* M. Morris and P. Patton (Eds.). Sydney: Feral Publications.

Gates, H. L. (1989). Narration and cultural memory in the African-American tradition. In *Talk that talk: An Anthology of African American storytelling.* New York: Simon and Schuster, pp. 15–19.

Giroux, H. (1988). *Teachers as intellectuals: Toward a critical pedagogy of learning.* Boston: Bergin and Harvey.

Greene, M. (1978). *Landscapes of learning.* New York: Teachers College Press.

Hamann, L., Schultz, L., Smith, M., and White, B. (1990). "Making connections: The power of autobiographical writing before reading." Manuscript submitted for publication.

Hardy, B. (1968). Towards a poetic of fiction: An approach through narrative. In *Novel: A forum on fiction*. Providence, RI: Brown University.

Holmes Group Report. (1986). *Tomorrow's teachers*. East Lansing, MI: The Holmes Group.

Macrorie, K. (1970). *Uptaught*. New York: Hayden.

Polakow, V. (1985). Whose stories should we tell? Critical phenomenology as a call to action. *Language Arts* 62: 8: 1–16.

Polanyi, M. (1962). *Personal knowledge: Towards a post-critical philosophy*. Chicago: University of Chicago.

Robinson, I., and Stock, P. (1990). The politics of literacy. In J. L. Robinson. *Conversations on the written word: Essays on language and literacy*. Portsmouth, NH: Boynton/Cook.

Rosen, B. (1988). *And none of it was nonsense: The power of storytelling in school*. Portsmouth, NH: Heinemann.

Scholes, R. (1985). *Textual power: Literary theory and the teaching of English*. New Haven: Yale University Press.

Smith, M., and White, B. (1991). That Reminds Me of the Time . . .: Using autobiographical writing before reading to enhance response. To appear in D. Bogdan and S. Straw (Eds.), *Constructive reading: Teaching beyond communication*. Portsmouth, NH: Boynton/Cook.

Stock, P. (1991). The dialogic curriculum: Students and teachers researching together. Unpublished manuscript.

Wells, Gordon. (1986). *The meaning makers: Children learning language and using language to learn*. Portsmouth, NH: Heinemann.

White, B. (1990). Writing before reading: Its effects upon discussion and understanding of text. Unpublished doctoral dissertation, University of Wisconsin—Madison.

RE: Structure, Class, Room ... and Technology

Carolyn Handa
American River College
Sacramento, California

*B*ecause this volume's subtitle is *Restructuring the English Classroom*, I thought it appropriate here to examine three words that figure in that title: "structure," "class," and "room." Much of the vitality in our English classrooms centers on those three words. Teaching that responds to the technological challenges of our time, furthermore, changes the structure, class relationships, and notions of an English classroom's boundaries. When we English teachers acknowledge technology in our classrooms and simultaneously try to understand the alternative social relationships it underscores, we begin to encourage social and learning situations that differ markedly from those that have come before. Instead of reacting against the inevitability of technology and change and harboring negative energy that we then displace into our classrooms, we who acknowledge, examine, and implement technology will ease education into the new century with intelligent awareness.

Structure

Structure occurs on many levels in the classroom. The very *physical structure* of the room itself is a form, as we all know, that affects the

I am grateful to Marlene Clarke, still a colleague and always a friend, for reading an early draft of this chapter and pointing out certain murkier sections where I still needed to wrestle with my ideas.

way we interact with our students and they interact with one another. Closely tied in with the physical structure of the room is the *pedagogical structure*, whether we believe in product or process, whether we like to remain the authority in the classroom or share authority with our students, and whether we structure our interactions with our students as a result of that belief. And finally there is the *structure of the writing itself* that we teach, what we expect students' writing to look like and the modes we expect their thoughts to fit into. Should the college essay always be linear and argumentative or can it be otherwise? All of these levels are deeply affected, revitalized, and changed completely when we introduce technology.

Something "structured" or something "constructed" is, as Webster's says, "made up of interdependent parts in a definite pattern of organization"; this definition suggests that all parts depend upon one another, not that all parts depend on one single part. The goal of all classroom structure, whether on the physical, pedagogical, or writing level, is to make the parts, the students and teacher, interdependent. This new sense of webbing and connection is what causes the new vitality.

Physical structure

Technology is a catalyst that causes us to think more about classroom structure. If not for technology, many of us would never have stopped to think much about something very basic in our classrooms: the way the desks and chairs are arranged. Classrooms in colleges and universities have been, I think, some of the *least* creatively structured environments for students, this lack of creativity reflecting the degree to which we unquestioningly accept one of the least vital teaching methods: the lecture. With its front-focused design, raised dais and isolated podium, the lecture hall seems built purposely to intimidate students and discourage any equal interchange between those students and the lecturer.

But consider what happens once we incorporate technology, in the form of computers, into the classroom. The very notion of row upon row of computers all facing forward toward a teacher dictating from a podium seems not only impersonal, but inefficient and disenfranchising as far as methodology is concerned (Barker and Kemp, 1990). Thus the computers cause us to think about the social implications of the structure we have so long taken for granted and we suddenly find ourselves playing with the possibilities of different structures, from elliptical configurations to pods (Boiarsky, 1990). English teachers working with computers know enough now to realize that a debate over a computer classroom's design is not only possible, but necessary because the room's structure not only *does* reflect but *should consciously* reflect the pedagogical goals of the department installing the facility (Selfe, 1989a). Computers did not cause the awareness we now see in instructors involved with computer classrooms and labs but they helped to make evident the weaknesses and implications of a structure that simply existed before, its very familiarity and tradition masking pedagogical implications that we have lately come to question: "Is the lecture the Achille's heel of our profession?" asks Robert Nielsen. "The ability to give a good lecture, once the epitome of everything most desirable in a teacher, has become education's white elephant. The lecture itself has come to symbolize the archaisms of drill, rote and authoritarianism — the worst aspects of an obsolete curriculum. This remnant prevails at a time when reform and restructuring efforts call for a new paradigm in teaching, one that involves critical thinking, creativity and participation" (1991, p. 16).

Since first teaching in computer classrooms I have become increasingly sensitive to room structure and its political implications. When asked recently to help design a new computer facility I was gratified to find that discussion of possible designs seemed to automatically include discussion of teaching methodology. Some instructors recognized, for instance, that colleagues with a more authoritative, controlling pedagogy tended to favor an elliptical or horseshoe design because it allows such teachers to walk around the room and peer over the shoulders of their students who all sit side by side either 1) facing the walls and not one another, or 2) facing inward focusing on the teacher at the design's center. Teachers who favored a collaborative methodology and the relinquishing of strict authority felt that nothing short of the pod design, where students face one another in small groups, would do. Departments installing computer classrooms seem to realize more and more how much that classroom's design reflects on them and affects their pedagogy.

Many instructors today want to set up a classroom that actively encourages students to participate in forming their own knowledge, rather than expecting the teacher to spoon-feed them. They recognize that if they want classrooms with this character, they will have to structure them differently, structure them so that students focus on one another, not on the teacher. In addition to face-to-face peer groups and pairs, the electronic classroom allows additional restructuring: a local area network in classrooms can encourage students to communicate with one another about their writing, can help them overcome the distractions and social inhibitions that hinder face-to-face discussions about writing. In many ways, these vital, new classroom structures exist as much for the teachers' benefits as the students' because in reflecting a more contemporary, participatory pedagogy, they also serve as daily reminders of the need to keep from unconsciously lapsing back into obsolete, authoritative teaching methods.

Pedagogical structure

Besides being a catalyst for discussing what exactly room structures imply, the computer has also caused teachers to begin reflecting seriously on their own pedagogical philosophies and the ways they implement those philosophies in the classroom. Our pedagogies dictate the way we structure the semester and define our positions as teachers. The computer allows us to capitalize on our stance, no matter what our philosophy. The computer in itself works neither one way nor the other, and in fact, can lend itself very well to reinforcing authoritative and rote methods of teaching (Handa, 1990).

Those of us, however, who shy away from drills and who work to get our students to value revision and consulting their own peers during this revision process have realized that the computer offers a tool to help implement more effectively a social constructivist pedagogy. For such teachers, writing does not arise in a vacuum because knowledge is a social act (LeFevre, 1987); we need to hear the voices of others combining with our own in order to come to know.

Because of the ease with which students can revise on the computer, it makes sense for the instructor to build the semester around a series of revisions, not just single-draft assignments, and to focus on the process of writing.

Depending on the sophistication of the computer facility, such teachers can implement on-line peer-group editing, synchronous class discussions of student work and assigned readings, and computer conferencing (or asynchronous electronic postings). One could argue that nothing about any of the above teaching methods is new or vital, but as Trent Batson (1991) has argued, meeting in a networked computer facility instead of a regular classroom and writing to one another much of the time instead of talking to one another, something not possible without computers, is invigoratingly different: "Moving to written interaction rather than spoken interaction — is actually not so simple after all. There are the psychological dimensions implicit in the combination of physical proximity and realtime written discourse[,] something about the electricity of being together but *not* using voices to communicate and *not* seeing faces when you do: there is the social power without the normal constraints. This creates a great release of energy that is not possible without computers."

Whether through synchronous group discussions or asynchronous electronic bulletin boards, computers allow students a new kind of opportunity to think their ideas through in the context of an ongoing discussion and to thus become particularly aware of audience. These students write for more than the teacher and they receive responses to their comments almost immediately after they make them. Such a rapid response, compared to the several days to a week or more we may take to return student papers, and an ongoing interchange, as opposed to a teacher's static comments in the margins, puts writing in the context of a conversation. Students find themselves asking other students to clarify, to be more precise, to give examples. Students' writing and their ideas in such a context gain a vitality not often found outside a networked classroom.

Writing structure

Technology will soon explode our very notions of what "proper" writing looks like. Cynthia Selfe (1989b) makes some important observations about the different structures of writing that surface once teachers begin running "paperless" classrooms, classrooms, that is, where all handouts, notes, and assignments are handled completely by the computers. Here student work begins to assume the dimensions that Richard Lanham (1989, 1990) foresaw regarding literary decorum. Students in these classes never submit hard copy to their teachers, do all of their reading and writing on the computer, and thus begin to take advantage of options unique to text on a computer:

> [Faculty] began to notice that the writing assignments students did for viewing on the computer screen were different in both form and content from the writing assignments they produced for viewing in the print medium. One of the first characteristics that became evident, for instance, was that students had learned on their own initiative to write text to be read on a screen rather than on a page, thus handicapping those students who printed such text out in a print medium. In screen-based papers, for example, students incorporated flashing notes and headings, boldfaced type, and highlighted segments

of text (light background color and dark characters rather than the usual dark background and light characters)—all conventions that do not print legibly in hard copy. In addition, students used formatting conventions that were screen-based rather than page-based, often using shorter paragraphs that could be viewed on a single screen, breaking the text into screen-sized chunks so that readers could more efficiently use the "page-up" and "page-down" keys as they read, and centering text within the window of the page.

A second, and perhaps more unusual, characteristic of screen-based texts involved the use of color as a visual cue to underlying logical content and structure. Students, for example, used three different colors to signify primary, secondary, and tertiary headings; used two different colors to "paint" contrasting arguments contained within a single paragraph; and used color-coding to identify thesis or topic statements and the evidence that supported these central ideas. These "painting" strategies are important because they go beyond mere decoration of a text to represent a visual revelation of logical structures. (Selfe, 1989b, pp. 12–13)

In other words, these students are not merely perfecting page layout while ignoring more serious matters of content and style. Their screen-based strategies are inextricably intertwined with the rhetorical presentation of their argument's logical movement.

Selfe continues, arguing that students composing text strictly for the screen "have invented and exploited a new set of literacy skills that their teachers never imagined," that they are reconceptualizing traditional assignments to mesh with conventions of the new technology. On pedagogical and other theoretical levels these students' differing ways of expressing their thinking cause Selfe to wonder whether other computer conventions such as virtual text—text that exists solely on the computer—and windowing will lead us to new conceptions of printed text and to a kind of conceptual ground we have yet to imagine.

Hypertext is also changing our notions of writing structure.

A hypertext is in some ways like an encyclopedia, a collection of writings through which the reader is free to move in almost any sequence. But unlike a printed encyclopedia, the hypertext does not come to the reader with a predefined structure. The "articles" in a hypertext are not arranged by title or subject; instead each passage contains links or reference markers that point toward other passages. These markers may be words in the text, keywords implied by the text, or special symbols. Invoking the link, by typing a phrase on a keyboard or sending some indication through a pointing device (or "mouse"), brings the indicated passage to the screen. (Moulthrop, 1989, pp. 18–19)

Based on a nonlinear method of organization, hypertext will allow different ways of creating assignments, commenting on assignments, and encouraging students' creativity to embark in directions never quite imagined before. Hypertext programs, for instance, could assist students in annotations and close readings of poetry or prose, activities possible before, but quite cumbersome to organize and present. Through one simple HyperCard program, users can annotate any word on the screen so that if the next readers point the cursor at one of those specially modified words, these readers can then see definitions and textual comments that the orginal user entered. Readers of such text will literally be able to visualize simultaneously the multiple meanings embedded in a single word of a poem; they could also see on-screen, again simultaneously, the variety of critical commentary surrounding a single passage or line of poetry. Two or three of the most sharply differing views could be shown simultaneously to give viewers a sense of the critical debates some controversial passages generate. Such HyperCard programs would serve to link a work visually to its critical history so that such a history would seem less abstract than it usually does to students.

More sophisticated hypertext programs allow the user to create a written document by moving from and to a multitude of directions, the "outline" of the text coming to resemble a complex, uneven web, a form quite different from the linear patterns of outlines with which we are most familiar. Such systems could allow students to forge links between words in a poem that all bear on one particular theme. A student analyzing a poem set into a hypertext structure would clearly not be thinking in a linear fashion and could organize a presentation of such a poem that would, again, be nonlinear yet coherent.

Class

Any definition of the word "class" involves notions of people, whether adults or children, separated into groups that are usually arranged hierarchically. Children, for instance, are separated into classes according to age and such arbitrary factors as intellectual and athletic ability; adults fall into classes according to economic and professional status. Sometimes we grant others status according to intellectual ability. We are all grouped according to sex and men have traditionally been the class with more power. Whatever the situation, class in this country involves the perceived separation among groups.

Technology in the form of the computer in the English classroom, however, helps us challenge some of our traditional notions of class divisions, whether articulated or not, and has caused a revitalization through the types of connectivity that have occurred. Stepping back to survey English classrooms in the very broadest sense, we see first of all a class division between students and teachers. But teachers have found that when they converse along with students on local area networks within their classrooms the sharp divisions between the two groups disappear. Unless they give clear identifying signs on the screen, teachers and their remarks are no longer privileged (Selfe, 1990, pp. 125–127). This interaction tends to neutralize any authoritative control the teacher might want to invoke. The brief revoking of teacherly privilege serves a pedagogical function. When students stop privileging their teacher's remarks as words akin to divine revelation, they are freed to think on their own and to arrive at their own opinions. By participating on the network and shutting off, however momentarily, their voices of authority and their own critical opinions, teachers have begun the first steps toward training their students in intellectual self-reliance.

But we can also see class divisions between teachers themselves, teachers and graduate students (or instructional assistants and aides), teachers and their administrators, and finally, K through 12 teachers and college teachers. Sadly, vast chasms separate teachers themselves. No matter how wrong this division, teachers in four-year colleges and universities occupy the highest rungs on the class ladder and seem to almost unconsciously bestow the most status on those at leading research institutions. Community-college instructors fall into another class and, sad to say, neither of these first two groups spends much time communicating with teachers in the K through 12 grades. I have found, though, that those English teachers working on wide-area networks tend to ignore these irrational class barriers between groups. Especially on an electronic conference called Megabyte University housed at Texas Tech University and participated in principally by writing teachers across the country who use computers in their classes, distinctions that operate to a very high degree in a hierarchically bound organization, say, like the Modern Language Association and the Conference on College Composition and Communication, are completely ignored. Participants respect one another not for their rank in a particular ivy-league university, but for the intelligence of their contributions to the several ongoing discussions of the conference. Some of the most valued members of the group are graduate students whose extremely intelligent contributions to the field of computers and writing are serving to move the field forward rapidly. Members also recognize that some of the most innovative work being done comes from members at community colleges like Northern Virginia Community College and Jackson Community College in Jackson, Michigan. Basically, though, people tend to ignore academic rank and school as a mark of distinction. As far as the field of computers and writing goes, technology has helped dissipate archaic, elitist notions of an academic hierarchy that many of us have become so accustomed to we hardly recognize them, and has injected a real sense of cooperative vitality.

There is even a class gulf between teachers and the very technicians who keep their computers in working order. Technology, however, has begun to erode the division that exists on many campuses between teachers and the technical support staff that keeps their work with computers running smoothly. Because of our attempts to bring the Internet to local community colleges and high schools, the network administrator at the University of California, Davis, and I have found ourselves working closely together, exchanging technical information, each of us supplementing the other's shortcomings in technical and pedagogical expertise (see below for a further description of this project). In our collaborative work on papers for panels and grant proposals, however, she has pointed out a fact to me that I have been blind to: the University has not traditionally recognized computer support personnel, technicians, as people worth supporting with grants to attend conferences or do research. Yet because of the growing use in the English classroom of technology like wide-area networks, teaching staff will need increasingly not only to communicate clearly with technical staff, but to collaborate with them on educational projects and to learn to think together about the type of education we want to implement in our classrooms. Technology is forging a vital new type of educational partnership and causing us to question distinctions that we would do well to re-examine.

The Seventh Conference on Computers and Writing has made perceptible the revitalizing of the field that has only just begun by the connections being made between teachers and computer technologists. The theme of the conference was "Making Connections," and the conference organizers specifically invited paper submissions that would discuss connecting the academic and working world. More than any other group of English teachers, those working in the area of computers and writing have begun to recognize that type of educational vitality that results when we begin to break down the barriers between teachers and technical staff, and start actual work together.

Teachers involved with technology, in particular, have witnessed exciting connections between some of these different groups mentioned above. They have found almost accidentally that the computer has fostered interchanges and eroded those artificial class barriers that universities strive so hard to maintain.

Room

Technology has also expanded the very notion of a "room" itself, traditionally and literally the four walls surrounding a group of students pursuing the same subject; the traditional room served to isolate those students from others so they might focus their energies on their texts, themselves, and their ideas. Because of technology, however, the classroom's four walls no longer bind it. Classrooms with the appropriate technology, rather than shutting others out, afford students the opportunity to connect.

The notion of a classroom seems to have shifted in the same way that the old formalist types of literary criticism have given way to the new historicist and social constructivist theories. Instead of being objects set apart and examined without consideration for the historical and political climates that gave rise to them, forms of literature are now examined as products of these and many more social and ideological forces. Likewise, instead of being only a place where a group can retreat from the world and think or discuss without setting their thoughts in the context of the outside world, the technologically linked classroom becomes one part of a web of many, and focuses outward by offering students a chance to link up, through electronic mail, with historical or critical material stored on data bases around the world, or with peers in other states. Electronic mail also allows them to form study or work groups with students at campuses very different from their own. The classroom now because of technology incorporates a sense of space, vast distances bridged, a web of connections. It is a place to look out from and connect to others. The traditional classroom focused inside its own walls; the technologically restructured classroom looks to the outside world as a matter of course. It is a room with fewer barriers, a room where students' horizons are expanded.

On Megabyte University, the wide-area electronic conference mentioned above, teachers constantly inquire about the possibility of setting up electronic exchanges between students at different campuses and sometimes post lists of students who would like to participate in exchanges with others. This long-distance electronic communication will soon become an accepted state of affairs.

Students at Babson College in Massachusetts and Skidmore College in New York have exchanged compositions and critique letters over a wide-area network. In the final analysis, instructors felt that the distance between the schools helped focus the students on the effectiveness of their written communication because, unlike peer critiquing groups in the same classroom, students could not rely on other conversations to clarify their comments. Both classes were expanded beyond their immediate four walls, and despite what minor technical difficulties were encountered, the technology worked to restructure and revitalize the classroom: "The use of a distance network to exchange drafts and critique letters between composition classes at different colleges creates a distance between student critics and student authors which, ironically, brings students closer together in analyzing and discussing written texts. Because of the increased understanding students have gained about the demands of effective written communication, a distance peer-critiquing network also brings students close to their own writing" (Marx, 1990, p. 36).

In northern California a group of educators at two high schools, two community colleges, a community college district office, a state university, and a University of California campus, plus computing support personnel in both education and local northern California corporations, have joined together to form a consortium aimed at bringing the wide-area research networks used at most four-year colleges and universities to the two-year colleges and high schools. By coordinating the development of instructional technology within the local community and extending the reach of this new form of classroom instruction to all levels of education, the Consortium also hopes to define instructional technology networking needs, identify the resources available for introducing new technologies into curricula, and implement pilot projects in local classrooms.

In one pilot project teachers have begun planning ways not only to encourage students to communicate long-distance with their peers, but also to team-teach a writing class where each individual teacher will provide a different source of information for the students at the two different colleges, and students will form working groups with members at each of the schools. Instructors will collaborate in presenting material on writing a research proposal. Then with the help of support personnel, they hope to guide students in exploring the resources of the Internet as they gather material for their research proposals. Students will also use the long-distance network to collaborate on writing and editing the proposal itself. Because wide-area networks like the Internet allow researchers and writers access to vast amounts of information from various sources, the instructors hope that access to the Internet will improve the quality of the students' proposals. The instructors also hope that such an assignment will give students a positive sense of the long-distance collaboration that goes on now for team-written documents.

Students of the future will think of reading and writing as activities that connect them to the outside world, of literature as an art that maintains connections with that world, and of all three as valuable precisely because "the word," for them, automatically involves making connections. Such an attitude would signify a vast shift from the outmoded, romantic notion of the writer recollecting in tranquility, far, far removed from others. The English classrooms whose teachers remain critically aware of technological tools and thoughtfully consider exactly what such tools imply for those classrooms will become a vital, linked community.

REFERENCES

Barker, T. T., and Kemp, F. O. (1990). Network theory: A postmodern pedagogy for the writing classroom. In C. Handa (Ed.), *Computers and community: Teaching composition in the twenty-first century* (pp. 1–27). Portsmouth, NH: Boynton/Cook.

Batson, T. (1991). "Our Enterprise." Message to Megabyte University electronic conference, 8 January 1991.

Boiarsky, C. (1990). Computers in the classroom: The instruction, the mess, the noise, the writing. In C. Handa (Ed.), *Computers and community: Teaching composition in the twenty-first century* (pp. 47–67). Portsmouth, NH: Boynton/Cook.

Handa, C. (1990). Politics, ideology, and the strange, slow death of the isolated composer or why we need community in the writing classroom. In C. Handa (Ed.), *Computers and community: Teaching composition in the twenty-first century* (pp. 160–184). Portsmouth, NH: Boynton/Cook.

Lanham, R. A. (1989). The electronic word: Literary study and the digital revolution. *New Literary History 20*, 265–290.

———— (1990). The extraordinary convergence: Democracy, technology, theory, and the university curriculum. *South Atlantic Quarterly* 89, 27–50.

LeFevre, K. B. (1987). *Invention as a social act.* Published for the Conference on College Composition and Communication. Carbondale: Southern Illinois University Press.

Marx, M. S. (1990). Distant writers, distant critics, and close readings: Linking composition classes through a peer-critiquing network. *Computers and Composition* 8, 23–39.

Moulthrop, S. (1989). In the zones: Hypertext and the politics of interpretation. *Writing on the Edge* 1(1), 18–27.

Nielsen, R. (1990/1991). Putting the lecture in its place. *On Campus 10* (December/January), 16.

Selfe, C. L. (1989a). *Creating a computer-supported writing facility: A blueprint for action.* Houghton, MI, and West Lafayette, IN: *Computers and Composition.*

———— (1989b). Redefining literacy: The multilayered grammars of computers. In G. E. Hawisher and C. L. Selfe (Eds.), *Critical perspectives on computers and composition instruction* (pp. 3–15). New York: Teachers College Press.

———— (1990). Technology in the English classroom: Computers through the lens of feminist theory. In C. Handa (Ed.), *Computers and community: Teaching composition in the twenty-first century* (pp. 118–139). Portsmouth, NH: Boynton/Cook.

Part Three
RESTRUC-TURING COLLEGE COMPOSITION

Still, the special conditions of the remedial situation, that is, the need to develop within a short time a style of writing and thinking and a background of cultural information that prepare the student to cope with academic work, create a distinctive tension that almost defines the profession—a constant, uneasy hovering between the imperatives of format and freedom, convention and individuality, the practical and the ideal. Just where the boundaries between these claims are to be drawn in basic writing is by no means clear.

—*Mina P. Shaughnessy*

"These Are Voices in History": A Dialogic Basic Reading and Writing Program

Deborah Mutnick
Long Island University

Dialogue here is not the threshold to action, it is the action itself. It is not a means for revealing, for bringing to the surface the already ready-made character of a person; no, in dialogue a person not only shows himself outwardly, but he becomes for the first time that which he is—and, we repeat, not only for others but for himself as well. (252)

—*Mikhail Bakhtin*

Nearly half the students who enter Long Island University in Brooklyn are defined as "underprepared." Like their counterparts at other inner-city colleges, their struggle to become educated is heroic, their resources limited. Ironically, the skills-based curricula offered to them as special support have often deprived them of the very experiences they need in order to participate fully in an academic community. Instead of engaging in active dialogue through reading real books and writing about feelings and ideas that matter to them, these students have been placed into developmental reading courses that focus on decoding textbooks and basic writing courses that all but sever the connection of writing to reading. The result has been disaffection, failure, and high dropout rates. This year (1990–91), in a major revision of LIU's core curriculum, we replaced Developmental Reading and Basic Writing courses with two semesters of a holistic six-credit reading and writing course (English 13/14), revolving around a theme, whole books, and a seminar-style classroom. What follows is the story of how the LIU program came into existence, how it compares to the University of Pittsburgh program on which it is modeled, and how it appears, so far, to be working.

The Need for Curricular Change

I first taught at LIU as an adjunct in 1986. Assigned to teach a required composition course in writing a research paper, I experienced the bewilderment that Mina Shaughnessy describes so movingly in her book *Errors and Expectations*. At that time, I had never heard of Shaughnessy, nor was I aware of the burgeoning field of composition. With my MFA in writing, I had been involved in "poetry-in-the-schools" programs, but I had never even taken a composition course, much less taught one. Equipped with a book called *Writing from Sources* and another teacher's syllabus, I entered the classroom with much trepidation. Like the students in Shaughnessy's book who attended City College under Open Admissions in the late 1960s, the students I encountered in English 17, the advanced composition course, wrote in a language I had never seen. My questions about how they had come to write such twisted prose, how they understood the world through experience and reading, and how I could learn about the theory and practice of composition in order to *teach* them something led me a year later to start my doctorate in English education.

When I returned to LIU to direct the Writing Center in the fall of 1989, after three years of teaching in New York University's Expository Writing Program, not only was I a more knowledgeable teacher but the LIU English Department had already begun to undergo major changes. Several faculty members had compiled a departmental handbook for instructors that includes an overview of composition theory based on James Berlin's categories, a range of sample syllabi, and papers and commentary by LIU English faculty on issues like teaching English as a second language and basic writing. Pointing to the department's new philosophy, a comment on page one of the handbook states that, "Because of the large number of second language and second dialect speakers at the Brooklyn campus, it is imperative that we respect our students' dialects and languages as different and not deficient." The mood of the campus, as well as the English Department, was different, not as gloomy as I recalled, not as ghostly. I remember feeling in 1986 that the students were barely present they seemed so alienated. How much my impression had changed as a result of my greater involvement — now I was directing the Writing Center fulltime, teaching one course a semester — is hard to say, but other faculty members confirmed that changes had indeed taken place. One area that was slated for revision was the basic reading and writing program.

By 1988, faculty and administrators agreed that the reading courses, under the auspices of the Developmental Skills program, were inadequate. The Director of the Composition Program argued that separate reading and composition courses unnecessarily fragmented reading and writing, content and skills, in contradiction with the university's aim for its students to become inquiring learners. In the reading courses, students read textbooks in order to learn skills like skimming for the main idea and identifying topic sentences. If the reading program was theoretically dated, the basic writing courses reflected no coherent theory or practice. Although some instructors had been exposed to the "new rhetoric," the quality of a composition course depended almost entirely on who was teaching it. Students would routinely pass through the three-semester composition sequence and the developmental reading program without learning to write or read; and the dropout rate soared. It was this latter problem of student retention that pushed administrators and faculty involved in curriculum design to reconsider the basic reading and writing courses.

A proposal for a thematic, six-credit reading and writing course was approved in the spring of 1990, reuniting reading with writing under the aegis of the English Department. Together with two other English faculty members, I worked on developing a theme and description for a pilot program for the fall, as well as a plan for intensive staff development to prepare teachers — both fulltimers and adjuncts — to teach the new course. We modeled our courses on the Basic Reading and Writing (BRW) course developed at the University of Pittsburgh by David Bartholomae and Anthony Petrosky (1986).

The Pittsburgh Basic Reading and Writing Course

Pittsburgh's BRW course reflects an intelligent synthesis of recent theory and practice. For example, Bartholomae and Petrosky explain what they mean by the title of their book, *Facts, Artifacts, and Counterfacts*, with reference to Steiner's *After Babel* and to the theory and method of BRW: *facts* are the conditions under which students function, their relationship to the university and the materials they encounter; *artifacts* are the student papers and performances that result from those facts; and *counterfacts* are pedagogical interventions that motivate students to revise their papers and "reject their apparent inevitability" (p. 8).

With BRW, Bartholomae and Petrosky want to reclaim reading and writing from skills-based approaches that reduce these complex socio-linguistic activities to transparent processes of retrieving and transmitting information. Influenced by the philosopher George Steiner and postmodernist theorists like Jonathan Culler, the Pittsburgh faculty want their students to learn to compose a response to a reading as well as to compose a reading; rather than coach students on scanning a text, they advise them to write in the margins of their books, checking or starring what interests or perplexes them, so that they can return to a record or memory of their reading instead of an unmarked page. Instead of testing for comprehension, they provide strategies for reading and writing, welcoming, not just acknowledging, the inevitability of different readings. They teach writing by teaching revision and editing; that is, they understand that the writer's struggle with her own material shapes her writing; and that the provision of ready-made forms for writing and reading discourages such encounters with thought and language from happening at all.

Bartholomae and Petrosky's most basic assumption perhaps is that reading *is* writing. Whether or not we write a response to a text, we must "compose" it; meaning is not given, but made, and reading requires us to construe meaning actively. However, it is only once this act of composition becomes stated, orally or in writing, that we really know what we have understood by our reading. Who cannot recall a moment of panic upon first trying to enunciate a new or complex idea? Two assumptions closely related to the interrelationship of reading and writing are that our ability to respond depends on how much authority we can claim for ourselves; and that reading is *misreading* because the construal of meaning through language always requires us to displace the original text. Meaning, argue Bartholomae and Petrosky, "results when a reader or writer finds a language to make the presentation of meaning possible" (1986, p. 11). Metaphors of role and performance permeate *Facts, Artifacts, and Counterfacts*: a writer must invent herself, imagine a reading, adopt a role of authority within the academy; comprehension is not a question of the possession of meaning but its performance; and certainty and authority are postures, features of a performance.

English 13: "Different Voices in History"

The LIU program, which is based largely on the Pittsburgh course, differs from it, although perhaps only in degree, in two important respects: first, we have chosen themes that explicitly situate our students in history and invite rhetorical analysis; and second, while we appreciate the metaphor of performance and the importance of the student's individual encounter with reading and writing, we would shift the emphasis of our course to a more social, dialogic interaction between teacher and student, among students, and between readers and writers.

Pittsburgh's BRW courses revolve around themes like work, adolescence, and more recently, the nature and uses of writing. Ours revolve around the relationships of stories to history and natural to social environments. As we designed our first semester of English 13, we reread Bartholomae and Petrosky's account of their choice of themes:

> . . . we have tried to identify subjects that would bring forward powerful and pressing themes from our students' experience. We want students to see quickly that they have a stake in the transformations they can perform on the ways they see and, thereby, participate in the world. (p. 30)

At LIU, we had not so much a different set of objectives as a different social lens through which we see them. Most LIU classes are a mix of recent high school graduates and older, returning students. Sixty-one percent of the undergraduates are over the age of 22; racial and ethnic "minorities" comprise 70 percent of the school population. The underprepared students in English 13 — educationally and usually economically disadvantaged — represent close to half the total population, as opposed to a much smaller percentage of the University of Pittsburgh student body. LIU's underprepared students are virtually the majority, not marginal outsiders; we wanted to address the historical reasons for their difficulties with reading and writing and their systematic exclusion from full participation in society. Thus, while we share the goals of the Pittsburgh course themes — to promote a participatory stance that invites change — we felt that for our students those goals would not be achieved through themes of adolescence or work.

One question we asked as we designed our course was whether such themes, however unintentionally, lead to a static, timeless, universal definition of human experience, dislodged from history. In our first discussions, we agreed that we wanted to accentuate both the role of story in reading and writing and a more dynamic, multicultural perspective. Our discussions led us to ask which stories prevail, how do our stories become *his*tory, and what socioeconomic and cultural forces determine that? What would happen if we used these questions, which are critical for students who continue to be excluded from the political process, to frame a course in reading and writing? We hoped that the theme, invoked by the course title "Different Voices in History," would not only motivate students but actually begin to challenge the conditions and practices by which they have been silenced.

By exploring how they and other individuals are historically situated, students in English 13 examine issues of exclusion, silencing, power, and inequality, while they reflect on their own place in society, the academy, and ultimately among other writers to whom they are beginning to talk back. Students in English 14 explore environmental crises, bringing what they have learned about their own and other voices in history to bear on one of the most pressing sets of issues of the 1990s. In a sense, in English 14, we are asking them to exercise the authority, fragile as it often is, that they begin to develop in English 13. That the majority of our students are unable to find *The New York Times* in their New York City neighborhoods when we assign them to bring it to class is a telling indication of their place in society. Both English 13 and 14 ask students to consider the possibility of transformation, not simply as an aspect of personal experience, but as a product of the relationship between individual and social conditions.

The first unit of English 13 on reading newspapers, for example, includes a critique of *Nightline* by Fairness and Accuracy in Reporting (FAIR). The FAIR report criticizes *Nightline* for presenting news analysis through the eyes of guests who belong to the male, white establishment. Students watch and write about *Nightline* and other news programs, reflecting on their own experiences and observations and confirming or disconfirming FAIR's assertions. Other texts for English 13 include

Harriet Wilson's autobiographical novel *Our Nig* and Henry Louis Gates's introduction to it; a novel about repression in Argentina by Lawrence Thornton called *Imagining Argentina*; David Malouf's fictional account of Ovid in *An Imaginary Life*; and James Baldwin's angry account of the Atlanta child murder case, *The Evidence of Things Not Seen*. This list has already been revised for ESL classes, adding, for example, *The Diary of Ann Frank* and Richard Rodriguez's autobiography, *The Hunger of Memory*.

More than the particular books, however, we have found that the course works best for those instructors who have understood and been able to communicate to their students the historical basis of the themes. Viewing issues of exclusion and oppression from a historical perspective, rather than as brute facts of life, created a context in which learning felt purposeful, meaningful, an antidote to the rote exercises that define so many students' educational experiences. Some English 13 instructors reported in response to a questionnaire that their students reacted negatively to the theme. "A bit heavy," one adjunct described it. "... It has dampened enthusiasm and spirit." Corroborating this view, a fulltime faculty member recalled that "all three teachers I observed said that their students complained, as mine did all semester, of endlessly reading about and discussing oppression." Two things strike me as important here: one, that we need to foster discussion and debate about the course and allow for multiple interpretations and approaches to teaching it; and two, that in this discussion I find myself in disagreement with the instructors' characterization—not of their students' reaction to the course theme, which I assume is accurately described—but of the theme itself. To me it is not a course about oppression *per se* but about the historical struggle of those whose voices have been prohibited from entering into political and cultural discourse. The relevancy of this theme to basic writers seems to me especially poignant and meaningful.

This approach reinforces my pedagogical aims, inviting students to enter into a dialogue and become active participants in history (the classroom as history) through their own talk, reading, and writing. The students in my English 13 section underscored their pride in joining in this larger conversation when they titled the anthology of their final, most ambitious papers (biographies or autobiographies in which they placed their personal experience in a larger historical context): "These Are Our Voices."

What shapes my thinking on curriculum design is an effort to approach problems both dialectically and dialogically. Let me return to

Bartholomae and Petrosky's description of the Pittsburgh program to illustrate what I mean. I appreciate their discussion of writing and reading in terms of "'alternities,' the possibility of 'freedom,' the assertion of personal and territorial rights" (1986, p. 4), but, just as I ask my students to do in English 13, I would place such claims in a more social context. Freedom, I would argue, is always contingent on socioeconomic and cultural conditions; to suggest otherwise to our students—that we can postpone the intrusion of cultural realities into their lives until some later date, or that "personal" rights can ever be asserted outside a sociohistorical context—seems dishonest to me. Despite its basically socially conscious perspective, the Pittsburgh program occasionally slips into what James Berlin has called "neoplatonic" or "expressionist" rhetoric—the view that truth resides within us and that individual quests for meaning yield the most authentic testimony.

Clearly, Bartholomae and Petrosky recognize the importance of classroom dialogue. But they seem to reserve another sort of dialogue— what might be called contentious or conflicted dialogue—for the last portion of the course in which the students, who up to then have been shielded from "the presence and pressure of the institution," are expected to make the transition from reading and writing as experiences of "self-possession" and making meanings of their own to an acknowledgment of the public nature of discourse. It is this social, or institutional, constraint that they suggest fosters for students

> ... a way of seeing themselves at work within the institutional structures that make their work possible. What we are offering them is not an affirmation of a person, free and self-created, but an image of a person who is made possible through her work, work that takes place both within and against the languages that surround and define her. (p. 40)

I would simply reply that this image of human existence is not a "*compromise* between idiosyncracy, a personal history, and the requirements of convention, the history of an institution" (p. 8, emphasis added), as Bartholomae and Petrosky argue, but a *condition* of human life. As Paulo Freire and Ira Shor (1987) explain, dialogue is neither a tactic nor a technique but

> ... part of our historical progress in becoming human beings. Dialogue is a moment where humans meet to reflect on their reality as they make and remake it ... in the process of knowing the reality which we transform, we communicate and know *socially* even though the process of communicating, knowing, changing, has an individual dimension. But, the individual aspect is not enough to explain the

process. Knowing is a social event with nevertheless an individual dimension. What is dialogue in this moment of communication, knowing and social transformation? Dialogue *seals* the relationship between the cognitive subjects, the subjects who know, and who try to know. (98–99)

Like Freire, Mikhail Bakhtin (1984) has given us a theory of dialogue that is at once descriptive and utopian. Bakhtin describes a profusion of social languages, emanating from differences of class, region, age, profession, gender, and so on, as well as a dialogic process by which the authoritative language of the family, teacher, and others in positions of power becomes "internally persuasive" language in what he calls our "ideological becoming." What he underscores for us in his discussion of Dostoevsky's writing is that dialogue "... is not a means for revealing, for bringing to the surface the already ready-made character of a person; no, in dialogue a person not only shows himself outwardly, but he becomes for the first time that which he is—and, we repeat, not only for others but for himself as well" (p. 252). Neither Freire nor Bakhtin argues that dialogue is a given; rather, it is, as Freire tells us, "part of our historical progress as human beings." Feminist theorists, sensitive to how dialogue excludes as well as includes, have addressed the question of inequality of voice in ways that are relevant to our students' tenuous relationship to the authority of the university. As Dale Bauer (1988) notes in her attempt to theorize a feminist dialogics:

> My first reaction to Bakhtin was to become seduced by his theory of dialogism since it seemed to offer a utopian ground for all voices to flourish. ... Yet Bakhtin's blind spot is the battle. He does not work out the contradiction between the promise of utopia or community and the battle which always is waged for control. (p. 5)

Rather than see English 13 and 14 in terms of a movement from the private vision of the individual student toward the language of the university (or any other public, collective discourse), I see an ongoing dialectic, indeed, sometimes a battle, between the student and the academic community. I don't believe that I can shield my students from institutional pressures. Such pressures—from the demands of parenthood to the workplace, as well as the university—pervade LIU students' lives, as they do mine. Nor do I believe that the university necessarily holds the answers for my students. Instead of a compromise, I see the relationship between the individual and society as both dialectical (an interaction of forces in which each term affects the other) and dialogical (an interaction between people, through face-to-face talk, or reading and writing or other technologies). I believe this dialectic between personal history and social history, or natural and social environments, as well as between reading and writing, self and other, is the basis of what we and our students do as active learners, as makers of meaning. The dialogue that ensues both renders and, as part of the dialectical process, already begins to change our myriad accounts of these interactions.

The Impact of English 13/14 on the University

Although it's too soon to tell what the long-range effects of English 13/14 will be on students, faculty, and the university as a whole, we can already document some changes and try to predict others. In the English Department, orientations and regular staff development meetings are held to train adjuncts as well as fulltime faculty to teach the new courses. Senior faculty members who taught the new English 13 report that, as a result of their experience, they have changed their teaching methods. Adjunct and workshop instructors have enrolled in record numbers in graduate courses in teaching writing. The workshops attached to the course are more vibrant, more meaningful, and better coordinated with the class than in the past. Graduate assistants in the teaching practicum have begun to apply some of the theory and method of English 13 and 14 to the intermediate and advanced composition courses they teach. Three tenure-track lines have been opened in recognition of the need for fulltime faculty to provide continuity and direction to the new program.

As for students, we anticipate that they will be better prepared for their other courses across the disciplines. In addition to being better readers and writers, they will know what it means to be students, to participate in a dialogue, and to engage in inquiry of various kinds. We imagine that their expectations of what a university education should offer them will change as they become more active, responsible learners. We also anticipate that retention rates will improve and academic success stories will become more common. Concretely, behavior patterns seem to have changed: attendance has improved—a real problem for LIU students, burdened with overwhelming financial, familial, and societal pressures; and English 13 and 14 instructors generally report that the quality of classroom discussion and written work is markedly better—students are more alert, engaged, and serious.

One of the most interesting experiences for our students is to return at the end of the semester to revise the first essay they wrote in class. The diagnostic essay, like our new placement exam, asks students to read a short passage from one of the course books and respond to it in a single essay, both interpreting what the author says and relating their own experience and observations to it. For English 13, we give them a passage from Baldwin's *The Evidence of Things Not Seen*, in which he writes about the hypocrisy of American leaders who show concern for poor communities only during political elections or times of crisis. By the end of the semester, the students have read, discussed, and written about this book in the context of our theme, "Different Voices in History." In revising that first in-class essay, many of them said that rereading it appalled them and made them feel they had truly changed as writers; most approached revision by discarding large portions of the early drafts and writing anew. One of my students, an avid reader, wrote a rather cursory response at the beginning of the semester, quoted in full:

> The message that Baldwin is trying to get across. Is that we can not change our race, we have to live with it. Not only do we have to live with it but we have to deal with it in the best way we know how.
>
> Sometimes we meaning monorities have to show violence not because that is expected of us, but because society pushes us in that direction. When it get to much for some of us to bare instead of taking a deep breathe and trying to find out where we went wrong, we sell out to the other side. The more of us that sells out the worst it will get.
>
> We have to stick together to help stop the disease before it spreads any further. It is out of hand now.

Despite the typical move of describing Baldwin as *trying* to get across his message, as if she has projected her own uncertainty onto him, she mistakes his anger as self- rather than outer-directed. This misreading reveals her own tendency to blame the victim (her own community — "we meaning monorities"); although she recognizes that "society pushes us in that direction," ultimately, she argues, resorting to violence is a form of selling out. Instead, "we have to stick together to stop the disease before it spreads any further."

By the end of the semester, the student assumes a more authoritative voice, integrates other course readings, and becomes much more specific about the "disease" of urban crime and violence she wrote about so vaguely at first.

> Baldwin is saying that the minorities only exist during a crisis. To the majority we cause problems but on the same token minorities are

the problem solvers. They separate the minorities into groups so we have nothing to do but condition ourselves. From there we are put into a never ending cycle of crime & drug wars against one another and towards other people as well.

The minorities are unrecognized or as Michelle Wallace said, "We are victims of invisibility blues." That is until we are needed for something. Whether it is to fight a war or election time: examples the only reason why slaves were freed was to fight a war that the majority wanted to win. Which ended up in a lot of blood shed and a high body count. The sad thing about it was they fought each other. For the elections it was vote for me I will give you low rent, better housing, better jobs and for the people on public assistant they will receive an increase in their check. Needless to say when they win the election all promises are forgotten. Until we the minorities are needed again. . . .

More than the assurance that she evinces in the second essay, the student has begun to enter into a genuine dialogue with the authors she has read, her implicit reader, and history itself. Traces of the first essay remain — "The sad thing about it was they fought each other" — but they are now contextualized in a way that authorizes her to participate in a conversation that includes but extends beyond her own experience.

REFERENCES

Bakhtin, M. (1984). *Problems of Dostoevsky's poetics.* Ed. and trans. by Caryl Emerson. Minneapolis: University of Minnesota Press.

Bartholomae, D., and Petrosky, A. (1986). *Facts, artifacts, and counterfacts: Theory and method for a reading and writing course.* Portsmouth, NH: Boynton/Cook.

Bauer, D. M. (1988). *Feminist dialogics: A theory of failed community.* Albany: State University of New York Press.

Berlin, J. (1988). "Rhetoric and ideology in the writing class." *College English* 50, 5, 477–494.

Freire, P., and Shor, I. (1987). *A pedagogy for liberation: Dialogues on transforming education.* South Hadley, MA: Bergin & Garvey.

Shaughnessy, M. P. (1977). *Errors and expectations: A guide for the teacher of basic writing.* New York: Oxford University Press.

Reading Strategies for Basic Writers

Sharon Thomas
Michigan State University

*R*ecently, I admitted to my colleagues that I have been borrowing teaching strategies from elementary teachers to use in my college basic composition class. I also published a descriptive list of those strategies and, during one of our recent weekly faculty seminars, decorated the walls of the conference room with large sheets of freezer paper on which my students had drawn sketches of an essay (magic marker and crayons), collaborated on a group summary (with color-coded revisions), and produced group-generated "maps" (not flowcharts filled with boxes and arrows, but highly creative and symbolic representations) of a text they had read.

I borrowed the strategies from my elementary-education colleagues. During student-centered, whole-language strategy lessons, they had discovered that students need some help taking responsibility for their own learning. Before beginning to read a text, students benefit from an activity that helps them call up information or past experiences that will help them make sense of what they are reading. This helps them make predictions so that, when they read, they can confirm or question what they predicted the text might be about. Ideally, the student-centered strategies would give students the help they needed without robbing them of responsibility for their own learning. Instead of simply assigning an essay, short story, or poem to be read, I needed to give my students some strategies for dealing with those assignments.

I started with pre-reading strategies. For example, one day I brought in four key terms from the reading assignment, and we had a contest to see how many people could put all the terms in one sentence that made sense. The sentences they produced were similar and remarkably close to the thesis of the text. For example, when given "Burma/Burmese," "imperialism," "British empire," and "anti-European" as vocabulary items from Orwell's "Shooting an Elephant," most students wrote a sentence about somebody being exploited but they were divided over who was being exploited—the Burmese or the British. "So read and find out," I said. And they did. The next day, they were eager to recount how their predictions were or were not borne out.

In another pre-reading strategy, I read the last paragraph of "Salvation," by Langston Hughes. Then the students wrote descriptions in their journals of what they thought had transpired to bring Hughes to such a miserable condition. (He had lied about being "saved" at the church meeting and now was further humiliated because his aunt heard him crying in his bed and misinterpreted his tears as tears of joy over accepting the Lord into his life.) The next day, those students who had made accurate predictions were anxious to announce that as soon as they came into the classroom. One measure of successful teaching is whether or not the students begin the class the minute they enter the room—before the class actually starts. "I was right. He did lie!" was undeniable confirmation that the students had become engaged in their own learning.

Now I use a variety of pre-reading strategies to capture students' attention before they begin to read because I have discovered that if I help them tap whatever knowledge they have relevant to the text, they read with greater understanding. If they lack essential background information, we try to build that information in class before they begin to read.

Sometimes, as a pre-reading strategy, I give students anticipation guides. I list statements that the author makes and put two short, blank lines before each statement. Before they read the assignment, they check off everything they agree with. While they're reading, they check off everything they think the author agrees with. In this strategy, students are able to compare their own beliefs with those of the author. For Fasteau's "Friendships Among Men," we discovered that more women than men in the class agreed with Fasteau. The women believed, as Fasteau does, that men have shallow and unsatisfying relationships. The men in the class disagreed, of course.

Other during-reading strategies include reading to a certain point in the text and then asking the students to predict what will happen next.

Then they read the remainder of the story or essay and compare their versions with the author's version. Sometimes I give them a "map" of the major points in the essay and ask them, as they read, to fill in all the supporting evidence. The next day, I put the map on the board or on the overhead and we combine all the details we've found.

Frequently, my students tell me they spent hours and hours studying for an exam, but failed anyway. When I question them, I discover that they made no attempt to construct meaning as they read the text. Proficient readers will underline, make notes in the margins, ask themselves questions, try to summarize as they read, and mark points of disagreement with the author. Telling students to underline and take notes can be helpful, but strategies asking them to compare their concepts with those presented by the author, comparing their version of the story with the author's, for example, give students the actual experience of being engaged in the reading process. Later, they can develop their own strategies for constructing meaning as they read.

So I've begun to change how I make the assignment (what can we do to predict what this piece will be about?) and I've incorporated some strategies for the actual reading of the selection, but the part I like best is what we do with the assignments after we've read them. That's where the freezer paper comes in.

Sketch-to-stretch is a good example. I usually pick a session when my students are ready for a less demanding classroom experience. I tell them the piece they've just read is to appear in a national magazine but it needs to be illustrated. Each and every one of them has been chosen to illustrate this essay. I give them large pieces of freezer paper. Freezer paper is sturdy because one side is plastic coated and they can draw on the other side with large markers and the ink won't bleed through onto the walls. And it comes in a box with a serrated cutting edge so that ripping off twenty pieces doesn't require scissors. After I've handed out the sheets of paper, I dump a collection of crayons, felt-tip markers, and colored pencils in the middle of the room. I remind the students that their illustrations need to be colorful so we can all see them when they're hung around the room. After some complaints about "kiddy art" and "I can't draw," they settle down to work. As soon as one person dares to use a felt-tip marker or a crayon, the strategy takes off. Battles ensue over who's hogging the green marker.

Once I divided the class into groups and gave them two very short pieces of writing. One, a piece about the game of golf, was developed through the use of examples. The other, a piece about salamanders and lizards, was an example of development through comparison and contrast. The majority of students who read the golf selection included in their sketches drawings of the golf balls, golf clubs, sand traps, water traps, fairways, trees, spectators, etc. In short, they illustrated the examples given by the author. On the other hand, almost all the students who illustrated the salamanders and lizards text drew a line down the center of the page and drew an arid region for their lizards and an aquatic environment for their salamanders. When we hung these sketches around the room and each student described what he or she had drawn, the message was clear. Using examples in writing does help the reader to visualize what the author is trying to explain. And sometimes these examples can be set up so that the reader can see the comparisons the author is trying to make. As one student remarked afterward, "I get it. You want us to write so that the reader can SEE what we mean."

Moving to another communication system enables students to generate new insights and meanings they can then synthesize into their existing frameworks of knowledge. Certainly, sketches enable students to see that other people might have different but equally valid interpretations of the same text and that they are able to respond to, react to, and benefit from other readers' interpretations. Sketches also force students to go back into the text to find the major point or event of the text and to decide what information is primary and what is subordinate, helping them to make better judgments about the overall structure of the text. Recently, a group of students made sketches of "Salvation," by Langston Hughes. The majority, by far, chose to illustrate the moment when Hughes was left alone on the mourner's bench, all the other children having gone forward to be saved. I could have discussed this essay and asked my students to describe the climax of the story, but a roomful of illustrations of that event made the point far better than a discussion could have.

After the sketch-to-stretch strategy, I move on to mapping. In my earlier attempts to use this strategy, I had shown my students examples of maps—flowcharts, tree diagrams, etc. Those examples proved to be too restrictive. Later I discovered that doing sketch-to-stretch first results in much more creative maps. We usually do the maps collaboratively. Each student brings in his or her map and then, in groups, they choose the best features of all the maps and put together a group map, on freezer paper of course, drawn with felt-tip markers and crayons. Then, each group presents its map. As an alternative, they make their maps on regular-sized paper and each group runs off copies for the whole class. In either case, the groups present their maps to the class.

Like sketches, maps also give students the opportunity to generate new meanings and insights through moving to another communication system. They also help students to distinguish between major categories and supporting details and to see connections that reading, highlighting, underlining, annotating, and outlining a text usually don't establish. A map is a graphic representation of how some ideas are subordinated to others. In addition, in order to make a map, the students have to read the text very closely, actively sorting out the relationships.

Recently, I assigned one essay to half of the class and another essay to the other half of the class. Within each group, pairs of students made maps, had twenty copies run off, and presented these to the other half of the class. The audience members had to write a summary of the piece after they had been given the ten maps and heard the ten presentations. Before they wrote their summaries, I gave them an opportunity to ask questions of those who had presented. Most students had questions. This activity gave students a better sense of how much and what kinds of information they should include for an audience who had not read the piece.

For Orwell's "Shooting an Elephant," I asked my students to work in groups to write a collaborative summary of the piece. We had, earlier, done this as a whole-class-dictated strategy on another piece in which I wrote down everything they told me either under the heading of "main idea" or "support material," and then we used the information to collaboratively write a summary. From this experience, we had learned that a good summary must reflect both the content and the structure of the text being summarized. Those students who seemed to excel at this first task became the group leaders for the Orwell summary. The summaries were written on large sheets of freezer paper taped to the walls. One person acted as group leader and another as scribe. The other students recorded the group's summary in their notebooks. We worked on these summaries for two days. I moved from group to group, advising, cajoling, settling arguments, and suggesting that when they got stuck, they might look at the summaries the other groups were writing. The second day, each group presented what they had so far and went on working, with my encouragement that they include ideas from the summaries of other groups where appropriate. The second day, I also gave each group a different-colored marker so that I could see what kinds of revision they did. The following summary (the quotations are from Orwell or from the introduction to his text) is typical.

> "In this essay, Orwell tells of a man in authority who finds himself compelled to act against his convictions." This story takes place in Moulmein, in Lower Burma, in the 1920's where the Burmese lived under British imperialism.
>
> In his early twenties, Orwell was sent to Burma to serve as an assistant superintendent of police. As a police officer, Orwell found himself to be an obvious target for the anti-European Burmese, which, along with seeing "the dirty work of the empire at close quarters," gave him several reasons to hate his job.
>
> One day, early in the morning, Orwell got information that "an elephant was ravaging the bazaar." He grabbed his rifle, with no intention of shooting the elephant, and headed for the other end of town. When he arrived there, he found a dead man who had been trampled by the elephant. At that time, Orwell sent for an elephant rifle, still with no intention of shooting the elephant. He wanted the rifle merely for defense.
>
> When Orwell and a crowd of people found the elephant, he was standing in a nearby field eating grass. When Orwell saw this he thought that the elephant was no longer dangerous and there was no reason for shooting it—until he turned around and saw a crowd of 2000 people. Though Orwell did not want to shoot the elephant his fear of ridicule from the natives overcame him and he pulled the trigger.
>
> Aside from all the divided opinion, Orwell was glad the man was killed because it gave him the legal right to kill the elephant, which Orwell had done merely to avoid looking like a fool.

The written summary is the next logical step after sketches and maps because summaries encourage students to move from a visual representation to a written one. Summaries are difficult for developmental students. They often randomly pick and choose pieces of the text and string them together rather than make distinctions between main ideas and supporting information, but starting with sketches and maps helps them write better summaries. As one student said, "I learned not to include so many details and just use the important parts of the story." Another student said, "Group summaries of reading assignments [are the most useful] because they help with ideas for papers and I find points to support the main point when giving the summary." Later in the course, when we start writing from sources, this ability to condense information proves very helpful.

Now, I have moved far beyond my original problem—how to get students actively engaged in their reading. Gradually I've turned to having students teach one another through class presentations. Sketching, mapping, and summarizing are tools both for achieving an understanding of the text before they present it and for producing materials to use in their presentations. I ask each group to provide handouts with its presentation. Thus, at the end of the unit, every student has a map or a sketch or a summary handout for each reading assignment. Sometimes I also ask them to provide a list of possible paper topics and to tell how they might develop these topics. Then, on the day we discuss topics for their papers, they all have a resource to turn to.

When the students bring in drafts of their papers for peer-response groups, they find yet another use for the strategies they've learned — they use them to respond to one another's papers. They read the first paragraph of the paper and predict what the paper will be about. They make a sketch of the climax of a personal narrative or they map and summarize an expository essay. If they encounter difficulties, they report these problems to the writer and suggest ways the paper could be improved. Now we have come full circle. As they become more proficient readers of the texts written by professional authors, they gain knowledge about what they need to do in their own writing to help their readers understand what they've written, and they are able not only to improve their own writing but also to act as knowledgeable readers and responders for their classmates' writing.

REFERENCES

Fasteau, M. (1987). Friendships among men. In P. Escholz and A. Rosa (Eds.), *Outlooks and insights* (pp. 186–195). New York: St. Martin's Press.

Hughes, L. (1987). Salvation. In P. Escholz and A. Rosa (Eds.), *Outlooks and insights* (pp. 89–92). New York: St. Martin's Press.

Orwell, G. (1987). Shooting an elephant. In P. Escholz and A. Rosa (Eds.), *Outlooks and insights* (pp. 45–52). New York: St. Martin's Press.

The Literary Experience: Reader-Response Theory in the Community College Classroom

Denise L. David
Niagara County Community College
Sanborn, New York

*W*ithin any discipline a theory gives us a way of thinking about what we know. It becomes the social construct of the discipline. Thomas Kuhn (1970) and others have talked about what happens when a paradigm, or a way of thinking about a discipline, begins to shift. He suggests that when a paradigm no longer allows us to ask the questions that we need to ask to further the thinking in a field there is a shift; that is, the theories of the discipline change or at least new ones enter the social construct.

It is easy to overlook the theories that guide us when we teach. Our grounding as teachers sometimes consciously rests on the theory we have read, but often it is formed by a subtle set of assumptions upon which our own teachers operated. However, when we let ourselves ask difficult questions about our theories, our teaching can take a new shape.

The nature of students at community colleges has forced me to ask difficult questions of my profession. The prevailing view of literature that has been shaped for so long by New Criticism suggests an emphasis on the text and the correct reading of that text, but it has left other important questions looming unspoken in my classroom. I may ask if my students have arrived at a reading that has credibility, but at the same time I know that is not a big enough question. I need to ask: Will any of these students read literature again once they leave my course? For so many of my students, the liberal arts courses they are required to take serve only as painful stops they must make on their way to "real," career-specific courses. They question the value of introductory literature courses and the importance of literature in their lives.

They see poetry as distant, removed from their experience, and little more than an intricate puzzle to which they must find the answer. My colleague, David Tobin, characterizes their attitude as "waiting for the Captain Midnight Decoder Ring" so they can decipher the meaning. Even if they arrive at the so-called correct reading of, for instance, Matthew Arnold's "Dover Beach," will they ever read poetry again?

My students are often impatient with themselves and with the texts they are reading. They want instant answers. Knowing that meaning often evolves after many readings, after much thought and after conversation with others, I must resist my students' call for quick gratification. How do I invite my students into the grand conversation — the talking, reading, and writing about ideas that are characteristic of those we call literate?

Rosenblatt in her preface to the most recent edition of *Literature as Exploration* (1976) asks us to reject the method of using questions aimed at preordained conclusions and to consider her view that "the most fruitful inductive learning arises out of the involvement of the student ... in a literary experience ... which leads him to raise personally meaningful questions ... and to seek in the text the basis for valid answers and the impetus to further inquiry." Rosenblatt is suggesting that the reader's response be the starting point for an informed reading. That is, we begin with a reading that is rich with personal connections, but move toward a reading that represents an informed opinion with supporting evidence from the text. It is not that a close reading is no longer important nor that the text no longer counts. It becomes a question of where and how the literary experience begins.

Rosenblatt distinguishes between two kinds of reading. In an efferent reading "a paraphrase or a summary or restatement — in short, another text, — may be as useful as the original text" (p. 86). She distinguishes this from an aesthetic reading. In an aesthetic reading, "The reader pays attention to all kinds of response involved, sensuous and affective, as well as cognitive. ... The symbols on the page are at best only partial indicators of the linguistic referents" (p. 88). She goes on to make the point that no one can read a poem for you. Accepting an account of someone else's reading she likens to trying to gain nourishment through someone else's having eaten your dinner. And yet, how often with good intentions have we, as teachers, tried to read poems for our students by overlooking readers' responses and moving directly to the critically accepted reading?

Using the theoretical construct of reader response has helped with teaching decisions in my introductory literature courses. I'm not suggesting that any reading is perfectly acceptable, but I am saying that if we ignore the reader's personal connections to the language on the page, we are doing justice to neither the text nor the reader. It is in the reading embedded with connections and associations called forth by language that literature begins to tap into a personal knowledge construct.

My teaching decisions have changed. I no longer ask comprehension questions at the end of a short story. I hear the warning of Donald Graves (1989) echoing in my ears urging me to beware of asking questions to which I already know the answers. I have found Ann Berthoff's (1981) notion of the double-entry journal to be very useful as a way to engage students in responding to text. It is a dialectic that allows students to have a conversation with the text. It encourages reflective questioning on the student's own reading process. I ask students to draw a line down the center of the paper. In the left-hand column, they are to record actual lines from a text — phrases or words that have stirred a response, a question, an agreement, a personal connection, or an argument. On the opposite side of the page, I ask students to explore their responses using their own language.

To illustrate how this is useful in helping to forge a connection between a student's response and the eventual writing of an informed essay about the literature, I'll share the work of one of my students. Shirley was a struggling young black woman in my Writing I class. She had missed a great deal of school as a child due to her affliction with sickle cell anemia. She felt underprepared for college and approached me after the first class to tell me that she thought she should drop the course. She had not had an easy time with the developmental writing course, and although she was willing to work, she had serious doubts about her ability to measure up to the other students in the class. I encouraged her to stay with the course.

Shirley wrote a double-entry draft after reading Toni Cade Bambara's short story, "The Lesson"—a powerful short story told from the point of view of a feisty young black girl who lives in a ghetto in New York City. The following is one entry from Shirley's double entry draft journal.

We laughed at her laughed the way we did at the junk man who went about his business like he was some big time president and his sorry ass horse his secretary.	I never read anything like this. It is down to earth. I can relate to it.

After her double-entry journal. Shirley wrote a general response to the whole story.

> I love the way Toni Cade Bambara wrote the story. I can relate to "The Lesson." It is nice to know that you can use black dialect in Mainstream English writing, and still be writing as Mainstream American English. I still have a handbook for black college students that was given to me the first year I got to college. I was told to write one way and that way was Mainstream English.

When Shirley shared her response with her small group, she found that she had read the story differently from two of the other members of her small group. One of the other members was offended by Bambara's language choices—the very choices that Shirley felt had brought her inside the story. The double-entry drafts allowed the students to focus their discussion on the specifics of the text and so their differences became a useful dissonance for discussion.

After the group discussion, Shirley shared her double-entry journal with me and we talked about the importance of word choice for an author. Shirley decided to write a literary analysis of "The Lesson." From Shirley's own response to her reading of the story she formed a thesis that made the connection between her own experience and what she was beginning to discover about literature.

> In 1988 I was in my first writing class in over twelve years. I knew it was going to involve hard work and self-motivation. I had to overcome my problems with writing. My main problem, I learned, was my African American Dialect that was keeping me from expressing my ideas. It was not acceptable for writing in college. Therefore, I was given a handbook called, "Writing in the Mainstream: A Handbook for Black College Students" by Edward O'Keefe, Ph.D. Upon reading this handbook, I realized my problem and proceeded to change my writing. Even though Dr. O'Keefe's observations were correct, I misinterpreted the handbook thinking that Black dialect had no place in any writing. However, since I have read "The Lesson" by Toni Cade Bambara, who used Black dialect throughout her story, I have discovered that sometimes Black dialect is a good choice.

Shirley built on her own response and moved from that to an understanding of how voice determines word choice in literature. She has come to see literature as something that emerges from an author's choices and decisions. The most formal choice is not always the best. Shirley read a commentary by Bambara on the writing of the story and quoted from both the text and Bambara's commentary to make her point that even though Bambara has her character comment, "But ain't nobody gonna beat me at nothin" (p. 616), Bambara herself is not uneducated and has made her word choice, as she herself says, to "strike a balance between candor, honesty, integrity, and truth-terms that are fairly synonomous for crossword puzzles and thesaurus ramblers but hard to equate as living actions" (p. 617). These word choices are the very reason that the story has rung true for Shirley.

Shirley goes on to recognize that if Bambara had made different language choices the story would have lost its flavor. At first, Shirley was not able to explain this to the girl in her small discussion group who was offended by the story because of the "vulgarity," but her own writing and thinking about the story have helped her to articulate an explanation. Shirley argues in her paper that something would be lost if Bambara's words were changed to what Shirley calls Mainstream English. Bambara's description of Miss Moore, ". . . and she was black as hell, cept for her feet, which were fish white and spooky" (p. 611), would not sound right, Shirley argues, if it were written, "She was ebony except for the bottom of her feet which were the color of a fish's belly and frightening."

Shirley has, as she says, "come to appreciate the value of black dialect." She has maintained her own connection to the literary text, using her own writing to further understand her own reaction, and she has come to understand the broader literary concepts of voice and word choice.

Shirley has gone on to complete the Introduction to Literature course, where she read and responded to such traditional works as *Hamlet* and *Death of a Salesman*, and she has also borrowed my copy of Toni Morrison's book, *Beloved*, which she and a friend read and "figured out together." She is now reading *Sula*, another of Morrison's novels. She reads them because she has made a discovery that has personal significance for her: "I never knew people wrote books like this."

Reader-response theory allows me to help students arrive at meaning without sacrificing the literary experience—the aesthetic reading. Meaning occurs first at a personal level, but like adjusting the lens of a camera we are able to see more and more of the picture as we share our meanings with others and negotiate these meanings with the actual text. My students make their own meaning, yet learn what makes an acceptable meaning and what does not. I have not thrown out the text, but have remembered the reader and the literary experience. My hope is that these connections will serve as the qualities that will invite my students back to literature again and again throughout their lives.

REFERENCES

Berthoff, A. (1981). *The making of meaning*. Portsmouth, NH: Boynton/Cook.

Bambara, T. C. (1972). The lesson. In D. Hunt (Ed.), *Riverside anthology of literature* (pp. 611–617). Boston: Houghton-Mifflin Company.

Graves, D. H. (August 1989). Presentation at Newark Schools Reading and Writing Workshop, Newark, New York.

Kuhn, T. S. (1970). *The structure of scientific revolutions*. 2nd Edition. Chicago: University of Chicago.

O'Keefe, E. M. (1986). *Writing in the mainstream: A handbook for black college students*. Sanborn, NY: Niagara County Community College.

Rosenblatt, L. (1976). *Literature as exploration*. New York: Modern Language Association.

———. (1978). *The reader, the text, the poem: The transactional theory of the literary work*. Carbondale, Illinois: Southern Illinois University Press.

Extending Our Concept of Multiculturalism: Lesbian and Gay Reality and the Writing Class

Harriet Malinowitz
New York University

Questions about who our students are, who we are as teachers of language, and the diversity of ways that we can enable diverse people to write and learn have become increasingly interconnected for the composition community as well as other parts of the academic community in recent years. Researchers and theorists such as Shirley Brice Heath (1983), Paulo Freire (1970, 1987), Ira Shor (1980, 1987), Carol Gilligan (1982), Pat Bizzell (1988, 1990), Linda Brodkey (1989a, 1989b), and Mike Rose (1989, 1990) have reshaped our consciousness of how different groups of people make meaning in a multiliteracied environment. Yet the same notions of "diversity" or "multiculturalism" that are being used to understand race, gender, and class difference have for the most part excluded the sphere of sexual difference. While lesbian and gay studies courses have started to sporadically appear in colleges across the country and even, in rare cases, in high schools, and while lesbian and gay scholarship is now being published in many fields, including literary criticism, there has been a virtual silence about heterosexism, homophobia, and lesbian and gay reality in the thriving, expanding, interdisciplinary field of composition.

We are now in the "gay nineties," and it's time we figured out how to create and position a lesbian and gay discourse among the multiple discourses that cohabit in our composition classes. In 1991 I am thoroughly convinced that all of us, gay and straight, must "out" lesbian and gay reality in our classrooms, but looking around I find very few sources of collegial collaboration in this enterprise. It seems obvious that a large part of the problem is that our institutions, as part of the society we live in, are themselves so heterosexist that the lesbian and gay teachers and students who might have long ago spoken out for change have simply felt too threatened to do so. Most schools and colleges still lack antidiscrimination policies based on sexual orientation. Gay youth who are "out" in school face verbal abuse and physical violence, raising their truancy and dropout rates (Tracey, 1990). Attempts to curb lesbian and gay art and scholarship get launched periodically, as do frontal attacks like the Briggs Initiative, which a decade ago tried to ban lesbians and gays from teaching in California schools. (It was defeated after a concerted mobilization of the gay community.) Lesbian and gay scholarly work has no cachet on a résumé, and is never even suggested as a category of proposal or submission for conferences, journals, or other professional publications—even when their theme is "multiculturalism" or "diversity." On a broader scale, people don't come out because, aside from jobs, they risk losing homes, children, and legal rights, as well as community, friendship, and respect. Many lesbian and gay people I know have lost their parents and siblings in what may strike some as primitive rites of ostracism, which are frequently practiced in otherwise "close" and "liberal" families.

I have been involved with lesbian and gay activism, performance, and writing for well over a decade. Yet I am also a lesbian English teacher who, until this term, hesitated to come out to my students en masse and to many of my colleagues—except in protected parts of the "ivory closet" (Escoffier, 1990) such as women's studies. I did come out to some students, usually those I perceived to be gay or progressive. I believe in the political importance of being out, because closeted gay people contribute to the conspiracy of lies that render the false impression that the species we call "people" is generically heterosexual. So I've asked myself what I have to lose by coming out to my students. Certainly in my relationship to them I am the one with the greater amount of power. The worst scenarios I can imagine, were the students to homophobically rebel, are ones in which I am reported for obscenity in the classroom or otherwise harassed. I know that the New York City colleges in which I teach are less likely than some others to support the actions of students who do such things, though I have no clearly articulated bedrock of safety upon which to rest this hopeful conjecture. If these schools do have an antidiscrimination policy including sexual orientation, it certainly has not been publicized adequately to allay my own fears or the fears of others—faculty or students—in the same position. But beyond the fear of such concrete retribution, I fear something else, and that is the loss of the warm, open, supportive relationship I like to have with my students, even if it is shakily based on false premises.

I can hypothesize that the closeted gay students in my classes remain silent out of some of the same fears. While some students have come out to me privately, or have implicitly come out to the class, none has ever explicitly come out publicly. However, many students have had occasion to make or giggle at homophobic remarks, and a few of them have chosen to write about their dislike of gay people. Those times when I have asked them to read and discuss a gay-themed article or essay, their responses have primarily been either to laugh, to express hostility, or, when challenged by an idea or a fact they hadn't known, to be defiantly skeptical. This has happened even in classes that have talked and written about a variety of other social issues and oppressions—classes of students who have expressed their outrage about racism, sexism, ageism, anti-Semitism, and other isms, from rhetorical positions ranging from the political to the sentimental. Usually, they will attempt to mitigate their own anger and derision by citing ostensibly liberal rationales; sexual orientation is "private," "nobody's business"; they don't mind what people do in private, they just don't want to see two men holding hands or kissing on the street or in the subway; they just don't like to see boys dressed or acting like girls; they have known a gay person at work, in school, or in the community, and "accepted" the person just like anyone else as long as the person kept quiet about his or her sex life; etc. Some of them are anxious to make it clear that they are not "prejudiced," and frequently deflect attention away from their homophobic feelings about gay people in general by invoking images of transvestites, transsexuals, and pederasts. By overlaying the real discussion with a hyperbolized one, they seem to feel that their negative reactions are justified, in that they are targeted at what are generally perceived as extreme cases of sickness and absurdity.[1] Others frankly acknowledge their prejudice, as if this particular form of it is understandable and acceptable. A *New York Times* article on homophobia several months ago cited research that demonstrated that "[anti-gay] hostility is far more accepted among large numbers of Americans than is bias against other groups," and that "while teen-agers surveyed were reluctant to advocate open bias against racial and ethnic groups, they were emphatic about disliking homosexual men and women. They are perceived 'as legitimate targets which can be openly attacked,'" (Goleman, 1990). Clearly, this discourse comes from and goes beyond the classroom, since lesbians and gays are virtually the only group left facing mass discrimination with no federally mandated civil rights protection. And as gay legal scholar Richard D. Mohr (1988) has pointed out, in the absence of that protection, complaining of discrimination can simply compound it, since the voicing of the problem publicly identifies the complainant as a stigmatized person and enlarges the sphere of vulnerability.

I would suggest that, just as black, women's, Latino, labor, and other discourses began to infiltrate university and high school curricula a couple of decades ago concomitantly with their politicized infiltration of mass public discourse, these institutions must let go of another group's hegemonic hold on reality — that is, heterosexuals' — as the refueled gay rights movement of the 1990s redesigns our conceptual landscape of human rights, realities, and demographics. At the 1990 New York International Festival of Lesbian and Gay Film, noted gay film critic Vito Russo described a conversation he'd had some years ago with singer and actress Bette Midler, a longtime gay-male cultural icon, in which she'd said frankly, "I've always wondered when you people were going to fight back and stop taking this shit." In 1991, the 22-year-old lesbian and gay liberation movement, bolstered by increased militancy around the AIDS crisis, and more recently the NEA crisis, is finally making its demands for civil rights and social countenance heard in the major media, in Washington, and in municipalities around the country. Yet lesbian and gay reality remains largely absent from our texts, curricula, and professional forums. The 1989 convention of the National Council of Teachers of English had only one paper dealing

---

1. For an illuminating discussion of "the sex hierarchy" — the vertical scale of social acceptability on which forms of sexuality are measured — see Gayle Rubin, "Thinking Sex; Notes for a Radical Theory of the Politics of Sexuality" in Carole S. Vance (Ed.) (1984), *Pleasure and Danger: Exploring Female Sexuality.* London: Pandora Press, Unwin Hyman Limited.

with lesbian and gay studies on its program out of hundreds presented (and the conference theme was "Celebrating Diversity"); the presence of an active lesbian and gay caucus in the 4C's has made the last several conventions of that organization slightly more groundbreaking. Most writing textbooks and essay anthologies for writing courses, even those attempting "diverse" or "multicultural" representation as it is now fashionably conceived, omit representation of lesbian and gay issues. I would hold that this is true even for those that now include sections on AIDS, which is inevitably associated in most people's minds with the gay community. AIDS is an issue that has become deeply intertwined with gay life, and can be fruitfully discussed that way, but to conceive of AIDS as *representing* gay reality is like imagining that hysterectomies represent women's reality. While it is relatively easy to be infuriated by Jesse Helms's blantantly right-wing campaign to censor gay art, there seems to be little corresponding outrage at the tacit censorship of gay issues in the college textbooks we use — even the otherwise "liberal" ones. A rare exception to the practice of topically obliterating gay life can be found in St. Martins Press' *Rereading America: Cultural Contexts for Critical Thinking and Writing* (Colombo, Cullen, and Lisle, 1989), which is laudable in this area for two reasons: one, that it recognizes gayness itself (not just homophobia) as a "cultural context"; and two, that essays are included in two different thematically constructed sections. An essay called "What Price Independence? Social Reactions to Lesbians, Spinsters, Widows, and Nuns" is in the section called "Racism, Sexism, and Heterosexism." At the unit level, heterosexism is immediately aligned with other, perhaps more familiar, social ills, and the essay title itself indicates that the stigma attached to lesbians has much in common with that of other women who are not attached to men, thereby calling into question the idea that lesbians are damned because of sexual proclivities alone. Richard Goldstein's "The Gay Family" is about a burgeoning social unit that most students are shocked to discover exists — since being gay is often equated with nonprocreation and the possible demise of the species — and in its section, "Alternative Family Structures," it shares space with essays on Afro-American family life, a mother-daughter relationship in a socially marginalized family, and friends constituting an alternative family structure to that of the biological family.

The focus on multicultural curricula has evolved in recent decades not as an abstract need to make education itself more diverse, but rather in the context of political developments and liberation movements in the nation and the world. As women and people of color have resisted marginalization and disenfranchisement, they have also fought for a position of inclusion in academic texts and syllabi. Beyond inclusion, they have pushed — with a considerable, though not fully satisfying, degree of success — for greater centrality and legitimate expression of their experience in the academy. Divisiveness within the composition community about the appropriateness of this inclusion has largely emerged from divergent notions of the place of ideology itself in composition classes. The argument at its surface level has been about whether or not ideology belongs in a writing class; at a deeper level, it is about *which* ideology belongs in a writing class, since new historicists, deconstructionists, and social constructivists have shown that culture is never neutral, unmediated, or value-free. Academicians who resisted ideology just at that moment when it ceased to be white and male were really fighting not just academic but vast social and political change. By the same token, any writing instructor who neglects lesbian and gay reality among the array of topics that are culled every semester as prompts and spheres of inquiry is committing, consciously or not, a very deeply culturally embedded heterosexist act.

An earlier version of this paper was presented at a conference as part of a panel entitled "Culture and Identity." Often, being gay has been construed as a matter of identity, in the sense of "personal identity," or "identity crisis." Yet for a society dedicated to constructing itself in its media, in its government, in its mainstream arts, in its advertising, in its military apparatus, in its religious and educational institutions, and in its notion of the family as unremittingly heterosexual, with exceptions categorized as "deviant," constituting that difference individualistically as matter of "personal identity" can be simply an amplified form of disempowerment. This is analogous to regarding being born a woman or African-American as some sort of congenital liability that inhibits one's social adjustment — one that, if one is lucky, might be overlooked or "accepted" by a tolerant, assimilationist society. The great power, however, of the late-twentieth-century lesbian and gay liberation movement is that in refusing the historic silence of closetedness and creatively utilizing the new "social space" afforded by contemporary work and domestic arrangements (D'Emilio, 1983), we are emerging as a "people" or a "culture" with certain commonalities, and as such we are becoming a politically viable force.

Anthropologists have attempted in various ways to define culture, without absolute consensus. Most contemporary definitions suggest that a culture is a repository of shared ideas, systems, and meanings that find expression in patterns of behavior and custom within a particular social group. It is the *ideational* component that defines the culture: what the people *learn* more than what they *do*, though it is quite probable that they will have in common certain things that they do insofar as they arise from their common knowledge. The linguist M. A. K. Halliday (1978) describes a culture as "an edifice of meanings—a semiotic construct" and maintains that "language *actively symbolizes* the social system, representing metaphorically in its patterns of variation the variation that characterizes human cultures" (pp. 2–3). Arthur C. Danto (1990) describes the way cultures become conscious of themselves:

> A culture exists as a culture in the eyes of its members only when they perceive that their practices are seen as special in the eyes of other cultures. Until the encounter with the Other, those practices simply define the form of life the members of the culture live, without any particular consciousness that it is just one form of life among many. (p. 33)

While we most frequently acknowledge that ethnic groups constitute cultures—in fact, it is our tendency to see them monolithically that leads to stereotyping and discrimination—women, too, can be seen to comprise a culture, in that we may share certain social meanings even across our ethnic groupings, such as the knowledge that our bodies are colonized, that we are both second-order humans and "Other" in patriarchal society, that we are expected to have a particular relation to child rearing, and so on. Similarly, lesbians and gays in the twentieth century have lived with an acute sense of difference within, and definition by, the culture of the Other, and have shared meanings at least since communities based on sexual orientation began forming around the United States in the 1940s (D'Emilio, 1983). We have known that we existed outside of the sanctions of society in those two areas where people's emotions tend to be most volatile: sex and religion. We have known that we could not legally construct the kind of families we wanted. We have known that we were perceived as immoral and dangerous. It was these negative meanings that lesbians and gays shared in the decades before the Stonewall uprising of 1969 that marked the beginning of mass gay resistance and liberation. Since then, these meanings have persisted, except that, by deconstructing them, we have also created other meanings, and still other meanings have been added to our shared consciousness as lesbian and gay bars, bookstores, plays and theater companies, books and presses, film festivals, resorts, periodicals, legal and medical practices, political groups and parties, caucuses, organizations, families, artificial-insemination centers, marches, and academic programs have emerged. In many ways, we are a submerged culture that has surfaced, trying to create a canon of information about itself. The editors (Hall Carpenter Archives Oral History Group, 1989) of a lesbian oral history collection write in their introduction:

> To uncover what has been hidden through silence, neglect, or marginalization, we needed to ask questions which recognized the complexity of lesbians' experiences. What are the important influences on our lives as lesbians, as women? How have we effected change ourselves? ... How do we grow up? What is waiting for us? How do we become ourselves? (pp. 1, 5)

The "out" lesbian standup comic Sara Cytron speaks in her act about her ex-husband, who also turned out to be gay. "I should have known," she says. "He collected musical comedy albums." Gay audiences laugh loudly. They know that many gay men love Broadway musicals. Not all of them share that particular obsession, but it is a familiar hallmark of gay sensibility, a cultural signifier. The underlying meaning of the obsession? Probably an attraction to color, dance, vibrant expression, flamboyance that is prohibited to men in western culture, and for which many gay men may have felt a suppressed longing.

In an important essay called "Literacy and the Lesbian/Gay Learner" in the collection *The Lesbian in Front of the Classroom: Writing by Lesbian Teachers*, Ellen Louise Hart (1988) writes:

> What is different about this process of becoming literate for a lesbian or gay man? The most fundamental difference is the need for particular texts that represent lesbian and gay experience and consciousness. ... Our lesbian and gay students need to know that they exist and that they exist in print. ... The claims I bring to this discussion of literacy are that the acts of reading and writing are acts of creation, not peripheral but essential to all education and all learning. Gay and lesbian students have special needs as learners in a patriarchal, heterosexist, homophobic society where their lives and experience are largely absent or misrepresented. (p. 31)

Hart goes on to illustrate some of the problems lesbian and gay students encounter within the current theory and practice of writing pedagogy. She points out, for example, that Peter Elbow's (1973) description of freewriting in *Writing Without Teachers*—"Even if someone reads it, it doesn't send any ripples"—doesn't quite hold up for the lesbian or gay writer:

> [A] student who is lesbian or gay may not feel that she can express herself freely and honestly and she will therefore censor herself. She may fear "ripples" from the teacher or even more from her peers in

the class. And so she will divert her first and best, her most vital idea, and the work of getting better at using language is getting undone. (Hart, 1988, pp. 32–33)

How many of our other theories of writing explode when we consider their ramifications for lesbian and gay writers? "Writing and meditating are naturally allied activities," says James Moffett (1982). For him, "authentic authoring" means "working up a final revision, for an audience and a purpose, of those thought forms that have surfaced to the realm of inner speech" (p. 65). "Ask for honesty," says Ken Macrorie (1984, p. 82). Sondra Perl's "retrospective structuring"—something she sees as a fundamental part of the composing process—relies on calling up a "felt sense" that "is always there, within us" (1988, pp. 115–117). Linda Flower and John Hayes (1988) tell us, "If we can teach students to explore and define their own problems, even within the constraints of an assignment, we can help them to create inspiration instead of waiting for it" (p. 102). David Bartholomae and Anthony Petrosky (1986) write about their innovative basic reading and writing course: "The subject of our students' study ... is their own discourse—their representations of the class's common material, the key terms and structures of their discussion and essays, the context they represent and imagine" (p. 8). Kenneth Bruffee (1980) says that his *A Short Course in Writing* "is flexible because it begins where writing students of any age, experience, or competence can—and in fact should—begin: generating ideas out of personal experience, perceiving issues implicit in those experiences, and generalizing on those issues" (xvi). Janet Emig (1971) sees parents, teachers, and, later, peers as the readers of "self-sponsored writing," which is writing about "self" and "human relations" (p. 92). And on it goes. A crucial question for us as teachers of writing is: How can we expect lesbian and gay students to become legitimate writers within these constructs unless we attempt to make the writing class an explicitly safe place for their "inner speech," their "felt sense," their "own discourse" to surface?

And a further question: How can we separate our effort to make the *classroom* a safe and genuinely literate place for lesbian and gay people from an effort to remake the *society* in the same way? How is the first possible without the second? And in what ways might the first enable the second? And vice versa? Most of the writers in *The Lesbian in Front of the Classroom* (Hart, 1988) mention a schism in their lives whereby they frequent lesbian and gay bookstores and literary events on the outside, yet are closeted (to varying degrees) inside the school. "Writing sustains lesbians," writes Hart. "Our 'weapon' against isolation and oppression has traditionally been the written word. For lesbians, then, the consistent culture has been the written culture. ... Lesbian and gay cultures have a unique dependency on literacy, and lesbians and gay men must be able to read and to write their own stories if the culture and the people are to survive" (p. 39). The gay British semiotician Simon Watney, who is best known for his deconstructions of AIDS as it exists in the popular imagination, has looked in some similar ways to the AIDS Memorial Quilt as an alternative form of representation: "To have this social map of America. To have Liberace alongside Baby Doe, to have Michel Foucault alongside five gay New York cops. In many ways it's a more accurate map of America than any I've ever seen" (Seabrook, 1990, p. 111). Lesbians and gay men have created countless print and graphic artifacts that render our experience as a people. To censor, either formally or by simple neglect, the entrance of these artifacts into the school is to promote a form of illiteracy tantamount to that which slaves experienced. For slaves, too, access to reading and writing was prohibited because it could too easily become the source of their liberation.

Thus, if we are interested in developing authentic cross-cultural curricula, lesbian and gay culture needs to be on the agenda. How to most effectively put it there is a question that gay and straight instructors will have to confront in different ways, since the element of risk involved is not parallel and the depth of knowledge and sensitivity to the issues raised is not likely to be, either. As Cindy Patton (1990) has written:

> How audiences and educators receive one another as "same" or "other" strongly influences educational endeavors. ... Liberals are for the most part willing to talk about AIDS and HIV infection and view these as everyone's problem, and possibly even as something anyone "might get." On the other hand, homophobia is still something that few progressive people will put on their agenda, and is rarely perceived as something they "might have." (pp. 110–111)

One resource that seems to me quite useful in starting to formulate a strategy is the Fall 1989 special double issue of *Feminist Teacher*, which includes five articles on AIDS education and homophobia. Two articles that I find particularly valuable are "Homophobia and Sexism as Popular Values" by David Bleich (pp. 21–28) and "Breaking the Silence: Sexual Preference in the Composition Classroom" (pp. 29–32), written by Bleich's five teaching assistants in a two-semester, first-year course called "Studying One's Own Language" at Indiana University. Bleich discusses the attitudes and perceptions revealed when the 144 students in the class responded to the following in-class essay assignment.

> Describe a conversation with someone either of your own or another sexual preference (lesbian, male homosexual, bisexual, asexual, heterosexual) on the issue of homosexuality. Give as many salient details as you can about this conversation, particularly how attitudes about homosexuality were *expressed*. (p. 22)

Bleich provides excerpts from the student texts that illustrate the majority feeling — about 60 percent — that "homosexuality was disgusting and gross — the most frequently used adjectives — and many men who did not actually advocate either extermination or gay-bashing felt it was excusable to either beat up gays or 'throw them out the window' if one of them made a sexual proposal to them." He found, however, that only one woman said she would react violently to a proposed sexual encounter, and none of the women advocated mass extermination. Twenty percent of the class, half men and half women, reported that homosexuality was against their religion, God, or the Bible. Bleich found a strong correlation between sexist domination and heterosexist domination, and makes the interesting observation:

> Insofar as religion [*sic*] depends on a central icon who is a masculine scapegoat, someone who "willingly" bears the guilt of the community and in whose name a group of men serve as intermediaries to salvation, it maintains both a psychological and institutional system of approval for the seemingly outrageous opinions of the young men in my class, while at the same time *implying these students' partial, but likely, participation in homosexual feelings*. From this perspective it looks as if the ease with which people use religion to support homophobia is made possible by the sexist functions of religious values to begin with. (p. 24)

Bleich found that "often in the women's essays, which also generally reject homosexual sex, some version of 'I don't understand' is used to describe their attitude toward homosexuality" (p. 25) and that a "tone of understanding and sympathy is much more characteristic of female than of male responses" (p. 26). Overall, he found that his students did not connect their personal feelings with societally or institutionally sanctioned homophobia, that they reified the concept of normative heterosexuality ("that's just how things are"), and that speakers from the Gay-Lesbian Alliance who came into class helped to defuse some of the fear and ignorance, particularly the popular conception that sexual activity is the constant and definitive activity for gay people, who are often believed not to have a life outside of the bedroom.

The four women (all heterosexual) and one man who were Bleich's assistants led twice-weekly discussion sections of the course, and write about their discovery, long after the course was over, of some of the errors in their process of designing and teaching it. Acknowledging that they raised an issue that they were unprepared to deal with, they question the chronological placement of gay issues in the course, the level of thought that went into it compared to that which went into other topics, and the nature of the in-class essay question itself. They point out that the question really addresses the heterosexual students' experiences:

> For gay and lesbian students, the question must have seemed horribly ironic, because the phrase "attitudes toward homosexuality" implies that the expected audience is clearly heterosexual; our question presents homosexuality as something "other," something that the writer should have an attitude "toward." For a gay or lesbian student to attempt seriously to answer the question in the terms we provided would call for a level of personal disconnectedness that the very classroom examination of factors of identity seeks to avoid. Indeed, the one student who had already come out to his class could only comment that the question did not fit his perspective. (p. 30)

They also reflect that the question, because it only asked the students to discuss homosexuality, suggested to the heterosexual students that their own sexual preference was normative, and not to be critically examined. They notice that, earlier in the course, the essay topic on race had asked students to describe a time when they had been made aware of their *own* race or ethnicity. This strategy of getting people of dominant cultures to distance themselves from conditions they take to be normative is one that, these authors later realized, could be effectively used to help students recognize heterosexuality as one possible orientation among several. The need to listen to different voices, to become informed about lesbian and gay issues, and to problematize heterosexuality (not just homosexuality and homophobia) emerged as important tasks for instructors as well as students of multicultural courses.

Recently, as part of a unit on "observation" in a New York University freshman composition course, I asked my students to read the first chapter of John Berger's (1972) *Ways of Seeing*, in which art historian Berger situates objects of art in their historical context. Then I had them read *Village Voice* writer Richard Goldstein's "AIDS and the Social Contract," and I had three speakers from ACT UP (the AIDS Coalition to Unleash Power) come into the class. The two male speakers explained that they were also in the newly formed group Queer Nation, and the woman, a heterosexual 17-year-old, spoke of being raised among many gay "uncles" who worked with her artist father, and who have all since died of AIDS; this led to her decision to participate in AIDS activism. By true coincidence, it happened to be October 11, which is National Coming Out Day, and so, caught up in the sudden and rare "out" moment in the classroom, I spontaneously did what I had long mulled over doing; I came out to the class.

An array of experiences and perspectives was then presented, including the message that AIDS is no longer a "gay issue" (if it ever really was), that teenagers and young adults of all sexual persuasions now constitute one of the two groups experiencing the most rapid increase in HIV transmission (the other group is women), and that the speakers were there out of concern for the students' own lives and the choices they could make to protect them. At the same time, in their concise historical overview of the AIDS crisis the speakers made it clear that during the early 1980s, when AIDS affected primarily gay men and IV drug users, the government, media, and medical research institutions were completely silent—and that this prolonged inaction regarding research, treatment, prevention, and services resulted in tens of thousands of deaths. It was only when AIDS began to affect those who were publicly called "innocent victims"—that is, those who were white, heterosexual, and preferably virgins, such as the sentimentally celebrated Ryan White—that the epidemic began to achieve national recognition as a problem. Unlike far smaller medical catastrophes, such as Legionnaire's Disease or the short-lived Tylenol contamination, AIDS was overlooked or actually greeted as nature's own extermination policy for the earth's undesirables. AIDS was thus presented to the class not as a *gay* problem, but as a *societal* problem in which homophobia played a large part.

I had arranged a spread all over the floor of posters, postcards, and stickers from ACT UP and Gran Fury, an AIDS graphic-arts collective associated with ACT UP. At the end of the class, I asked the students to pick up whatever interested them, and to write about their observations of one piece of graphic art. In their essays they wrote about what they saw in the posters, but it was contextualized, they said, in a way that it never would have been before that ACT UP visit and discussion; they insisted on writing about the social context of AIDS and homophobia, too. Many of the students wrote about putting the posters—which contained vivid gay and anti-Cardinal O'Connor imagery—up on the walls of their dorm rooms. They wrote about the reactions the posters had elicited, and the arguments they had gotten into with friends and family. Several reported having their posters slashed or removed, and one, speaking with his floor's residence assistant, found out that this was the second gay poster-slashing that had occurred recently in the dorm. (He and the RA subsequently planned a dorm-wide forum on homophobia.) Several of them told me privately or wrote in their journals that this was the first time they had ever sat in a room with gay people talking about being gay, and that it had been one of the most "awareness-raising" events of their lives. Others wrote in their meta-texts that the double take they had done on their own assumptions had had an impact on their writing, in the sense that they had learned in a very pointed way what it meant to re-envision their own ideas and question where they came from. Many of them expressed the emphatic belief that these topics—both AIDS and gay life—should be raised in other classes. While I would like to do further follow-up on why the inclusion of these topics impressed them so much, I would hypothesize for now that they were reacting to the sudden realization of presence where they had previously encountered an informational void, to real people where there had been abstractions, to legitimacy where there had been taboo.

I also had speakers from ACT UP come to my developmental ESL writing class at Hunter College. I expected greater resistance there, and was surprised to find that, with a few exceptions, the guests were received with interest and appreciation, even if their message was not considered altogether acceptable. Because those students were relatively new immigrants to this country and many were devoutly Catholic, because they were struggling with English and were even further removed from radical New York discourses than were my NYU students, who came from across the United States, I took cowardly recourse in not coming out to them, and asked the speakers to try to make militant points using accessible and unthreatening language—which they did quite impressively. Though some of the students were shy about asking questions of the speakers themselves, they showered many upon me the following day. I found that I didn't have to answer the questions myself; the class became a forum in which concepts about AIDS and homosexuality were tested, refuted, and examined. Drawing on the information from the ACT UP talk—which in this case had been presented by another group of three, who had been factual but less ideological than the first group—I gave them a choice of questions to write about, trying to see what connections and inferences they might draw themselves. One was:

> In the first years of the AIDS epidemic (1981–1985), the people most
> affected by the virus were gay men. During that time, almost no
> research or public attention was devoted to the crisis. What reasons
> can you think of to explain this?

One student said that she didn't understand why the fact that they
were gay should matter, since gays have constitutionally protected
rights just like everyone else, and equal opportunities for legal and
medical justice. Others leaped in to explain how far this was from the
case. Another said she wasn't sure what kind of research had been
done during the early years of other diseases, so she wasn't sure how
AIDS fit in. This led to a discussion about speculative writing and the
language of conjecture. Many students were particularly pleased about
the drift this discussion took because it addressed that age-old question,
"How will this help me pass the final exam?" By critically exploring
what they didn't know about the AIDS question using the little bit that
they did know, they realized that if you're asked a question you don't
have too much information about, you can speculate!

Some students, speculating that the Reagan administration's silence
on AIDS during the first half of the 1980s was based on the hope that
gays would just die off without outside intervention, noted the grim
irony that because the straight world ignored the crisis, the crisis
spread to them. One student from Cyprus, after boldly documenting
homophobic visions of gay men through her own eyes, her husband's
eyes, and what she saw as society's eyes, went on to write:

> Maybe people thought that if they let Gay men die from Aids, then
> the disease Aids would had been destroyed with them and that Gay
> men who were alive, would stop having sexual affairs with other men.
> Because of that, men would be happy and not feeling embarrassed
> anymore.
> But I guess that we can't ignore Gay men, because they are part of
> our society. Even if we do not approve them, we have to live with
> them and try to think that they are human beings like we are, but
> with different needs, and that they have the right to be what they
> want to be.
> If people made the research back in 1981, maybe today we would
> have a cure for Aids. We see that Aids began with Gay men but it
> continue to spread rapidly between other people too. And who's fault
> this is? I guess the fault was ours, because we thought that it was a
> problem for Gay men to solve and not a problem for the society to
> solve.
> I wish that someday soon, people will understand that they have to
> be united as a society and that they should help each other also to
> solve problems.

While student texts frequently conclude on utopian notes such as this, I feel that the call for unity is, in this case, logically supported by the writer's realization of how what happens to one marginalized and seemingly insignificant part of society can have cataclysmic effects on the whole — including the dominant part whose smug complacence proved to be its ultimate folly. "Society" is not, here, just a faceless blob, but a conglomerate composed of different strands of membership who would do well to recognize their interdependence.

Another choice was to write about the symbol of the pink triangle that ACT UP has adopted as its most well-known graphic image, accompanied by the words "Silence = Death." One of the speakers had explained that this image was appropriated from the inverted pink triangle that gays were forced to wear in Hitler's Germany and in concentration camps. I gave the students the following question:

> The phrase "Silence = Death" has become an important symbol for the gay community. Explain why you do or don't think it's a useful one.

The question was a little confusing because the symbol had been explained as a central tenet of AIDS, not gay, activism. But I was asking the students to speculate about why so many gay people were drawn to it. One Japanese student begins with great energy:

> In my opinion, "Silence=Death" is an excellent symbol for the gay community. It is so realistic. People must speak out in order to acquire their needs.

He goes on to predictably describe the great freedoms available to the American people, with the caveat that we must use these opportunities wisely in order to benefit from them. Then he turns his attention to the situation of gay people:

> Unfortunately, gay people are not socially accepted to some people in some communities, including myself. The government never wanted to do anything for gay people since couple of years ago. For some gay people, it is a matter of their lives. In a sense, the government is denying the gay people's rights to live. Even the criminals in jails have their rights enforced. There is no reason for gay people to keep silence.

Then, in a surprising way, he inserts himself into the discussion — which, like that of many of the other students, has until now been directed outward, toward that vast entity called "society":

Personally, I don't like gay people. However, they should speak out and work hard to convince people like me. I have an ear to listen and eye to see the truth. I do admire people fighting for their rights. The symbol strongly tell us they are fighting for their life. It is simple and convincing.

Ironically, there are a lot of gay people dying while others fighting for their right. The symbol could fall into any community where there is AIDS. However, it is much convincing for gay people to hoist the symbol, who are not really accepted in this community yet.

This student text struck me with its "Try me" challenge, its suggestion that the ACT UP speakers had convinced him that he could be convinced. This, it seemed to me, was an important step beyond a frequent male homophobic conviction (as documented by David Bleich) that to yield an iota of cynicism about homosexuality is to risk being drawn into that pit where homosexuality becomes all too personally plausible.

These student texts struck me as being among those that suggested avenues of possibility, ways that we can begin to bridge huge and vastly emotional gaps of belief and experience. Of course, not all the students were even this open. Yet I did notice that many of their revisions indicated the influence of the serious and reflective peer discussion of their classmates' earlier drafts. Perhaps certain truths from Stanley Milgram's psychological experiments are at play here — that people are less likely to behave cruelly, even when they believe they "should," when they are in the presence of peers who defy the pressure to conform to expectations; and that when directly confronted with the object of their actions, people are also far more likely to abdicate the cruel behavior that they believe an authority desires of them than when that object is invisible and, to a certain extent, imaginary.

How, then, knowing some of the predictable obstacles, are we to effectively introduce lesbian and gay issues into our writing classes? I have several recommendations for preparation and implementation:

1. Learn about lesbian and gay people. This is especially vital if you're not one yourself, but pertinent even if you are. Most of us are ignorant about much of our own history and culture, of our rapidly changing politics and demographics. Straight people have even greater gulfs of knowledge, fears, misconceptions. If you live in or near a city that has one, go to a lesbian and gay, or women's, bookstore and browse for a couple of hours. An increasing number of nonspecialized bookstores have "gay" sections. Look through the periodicals and anthologies. Think

about which essays might be useful to include in your syllabus. Go to lesbian and gay cultural events on your campus — lectures, forums, literary readings, plays, films. Contact the campus's Lesbian and Gay Alliance, and ask for suggested readings and other leads. A women's-studies program may also be or lead to a good source. Check out sessions on lesbian and gay issues at professional conferences and contact the lesbian and gay caucuses of the MLA, the 4C's, the National Women's Studies Association, etc. Get your library to subscribe to national lesbian and gay publications like *Out/Look* (published quarterly, 2940 16th Street, Suite 319, San Francisco, CA 94103), *Outweek* (published weekly, 159 West 25th Street, New York, NY 10001), and *Gay Community News* (published weekly, 62 Berkeley Street, Boston, MA 02116). The annual *New York City Pride Guide* is published in May of each year for Gay and Lesbian Pride and History Month, and provides comprehensive listings of regional and national resources (Pride Publishing, Inc., 568 Broadway, #1104, New York, NY 10012).

2. Experiment. Learn by trial and error as Bleich and his assistants did, with reflection and discussion. Encourage your colleagues to do the same, and exchange narratives about what happened.

3. Use the techniques you would otherwise use for helping students to think critically. The whole process movement of composition studies has helped us learn that strategies such as questioning, problematizing, active listening, peer interaction, using explora-tory or speculative writing, journal writing, freewriting, recon-ceptualization of perspective through the use of multiple drafts, and deconstructing arguments are all useful in helping students achieve critical insight and transcend facile assumptions.

4. Find out about the issues that are of critical importance in the lesbian and gay community and have your students write about them. Beyond homophobia and AIDS, there is the whole area of legal entitlement and civil rights — including housing, jobs, custody and adoption, domestic partnership, health insurance, bereavement leave, immigration policy, sodomy laws, and the military, including increasing campus resistance to ROTC's discriminatory rules. There is the rise of lesbian and gay parent-hood and the ways that the concept of the family itself is changing (including an important legal redefinition in New York City). The new controversy over "outing" — whether or

not it's ethical for the gay community to drag celebrities and politicians publicly out of the closet—will find favor with long-term fans of abortion and capital punishment as topics for infinite argument. There is the whole question of how lesbians and gays are portrayed in the media, from news coverage to depiction in arts and entertainment. When the popular television show *thirtysomething* introduced a gay character and showed him in bed with his lover last year, a large number of the show's sponsors pulled out. The character was not seen again all season. The Gay and Lesbian Alliance Against Defamation (GLAAD), with chapters in several cities, is an excellent source of information about media issues, and publishes a newsletter. (GLAAD is also involved with promoting lesbian/gay visibility in textbooks and curricula.) Queer Nation, a direct-action group dedicated to fighting homophobia, is another new organization with new chapters constantly forming throughout the United States and in several other countries. Gay bashing is on the rise; according to a leaflet prepared by the New York City Gay/Lesbian Anti-Violence Project (1990), it is the fastest-rising bias crime in New York, with lesbians and gays seven times more likely to be victims of bias-related assaults than any other group, a 390 percent increase of reported anti-gay crimes from 1984 to 1989, and more than 80 percent of all gay bashings being perpetrated by people 25 years old or younger. (Two very useful sources of information in this area are the NYC Gay/Lesbian Anti-Violence Project and the Pink Panthers, a newly formed organization that patrols gay neighborhoods to defend the community against violent attacks.) In June 1990, demonstrators marching through the Village to protest anti-lesbian and gay violence included in their demands enforcement of the regulation that the "Multi-Cultural Diversity" program of the Board of Education include gay and lesbian topics. Education is seen as key to stopping violence; as ACT UP says, silence equals death. If you don't live in a city with active gay organizations, you can still obtain newsletters from organizations in other cities that will keep you updated about what is happening. One way we can all make our task easier is to urge publishers to simply include a reasonable selection of gay and lesbian material in their freshman writing course anthologies.

5. Be prepared to answer religious arguments. There are lesbian

and gay religious observers everywhere; homophobes have no monopoly on spiritual truth, and this country is predicated on the belief that religious ideas should not trample on civil liberties and the pursuit of happiness. Metropolitan Community Church (208 West 13th Street, New York, NY 10014) is a gay church with branches in many parts of the country; there are numerous other gay churches and synagogues, too, that are likely to have resources you can use and people you can speak with. William Sloane Coffin, former minister at Riverside Church in Manhattan, wrote an excellent sermon on homosexuality which he delivered to his congregation in 1981. I have found that this sermon gives religious objectors pause because it enters into their own discourse, not dismissing the wisdom of the Bible but raising questions about its interpretation and the way certain prohibitions have become obsolete while others haven't. Copies of this text should be made widely available for classroom use, or for use on an ad hoc basis with students citing biblical support for homophobia. (They are available through Riverside Church.) Religious objectors are often responsive to the perspective (over which lesbian and gay academics and activists are divided) that sexual orientation is not necessarily. a *preference* — that is, something that is chosen — but a more pervasive condition, like race or gender. Most important, human contact may get even those most entrenched in the authority of the church or Bible to reconsider in some form. When I have come out to students who "disapprove" of homosexuality on religious grounds, I have found them more likely to rethink what they believe to be God's injunction than to rethink me. This leads to:

6. Bring lesbians and gay men into the class as speakers. Getting students to have actual contact with gay people is probably the most significant thing you can do to begin to change their concepts and attitudes. The net result of years of silence and persistent closetedness is that many heterosexual students lack any sense of a real gay person. Often the only gay people they *think* they know are those they have identified because they fit their stereotypes. Hearing gay people talk about being gay and having their questions answered are frequently reality-altering events for straight and gay students alike. Many colleges have a lesbian and gay alliance of some sort, and they often have speakers' bureaus (they will probably be glad to visit your high

school, too). They will also have other contacts and information. Queer Nation also has a speakers' bureau that is available to schools.

Bakhtin (1975, 1981) has said that "language . . . lies on the borderline between oneself and the other. The word in language is half someone else's" (p. 293). Lesbians and gays have always lived with the voices of heterosexuals, but the reverse has not been true. The absence of a dialogue at the fuzzy border where our discourses meet has consigned us all to a more limited literacy than we deserve. If we believe in some of the central tenets of contemporary writing theory—that writing is a process rooted in the way we think, that it is about making meaning and constructing knowledge, that it is about seeing and seeing again, that it serves heuristic as well as performance purposes, that it calls upon all of our interdisciplinary faculties—then the composition class is an enormously appropriate place for our students and ourselves to create a new matrix of literacy, multicultural education, and personhood.

REFERENCES

Bakhtin, M. M. (1981). *The dialogic imagination.* (C. Emerson and M. Holquist, Trans.). (M. Holquist, Ed.). Austin: University of Texas Press. (Original work published 1975)

Bartholomae, D., and Petrosky, A. (1986). *Facts, artifacts and counterfacts: Theory and method for a reading and writing course.* Portsmouth, NH: Boynton/Cook.

Berg, A., Kowaleski, J., Le Guin, C., Weinauer, E., and Wolfe, E. A. (1989). Breaking the silence: sexual preference in the composition classroom. *Feminist Teacher* 4: 29−32.

Berger, J. (1973). *Ways of seeing.* London and New York: British Broadcasting Corporation and Penguin.

Bizzell, P. (1988). Arguing about literacy. *College English* 50:2: 141−153.

———— (1990). Beyond anti-foundationalism to rhetorical authority: Problems defining "cultural literacy." *College English* 52:6: 661−675.

Bleich, D. (1989, Fall). Homophobia and sexism as popular values. *Feminist Teacher* 4: 21−28.

Brodkey, L. (1989). On the subjects of class and gender in "The literacy letters." *College English* 51:2: 125−141.

———— (1989). Transvaluing difference. *College English* 51:6: 597−601.

Bruffee, K. (1980). *A short course in writing* (2nd ed.). Cambridge: Winthrop.

Bruner, J. (1986). *Actual minds, possible worlds.* Cambridge MA: Harvard University Press.

Coffin, W. S., Jr. (July 1981). "Homosexuality." Sermon delivered at Riverside Church, New York City.

Colombo, G., Cullen, R., and Lisle, B. (Eds.). (1989). *Rereading America: Cultural contexts for critical thinking and writing*. New York: St. Martin's Press.

Danto, A. C. (1990). Inventing innocence. [Review of *Gone primitive*, by Marianna Torgovnick.] *The New York Times Book Review*, June 24, p. 33.

D'Emilio, J. (1983). Capitalism and gay identity. In Snitow, A., Stansell, C., and Thompson, S. (Eds.), *Powers of desire: the politics of sexuality* (pp. 100–113). New York: Monthly Review Press.

Elbow, P. (1973). *Writing without teachers*. New York: Oxford University Press.

Emig, J. (1971). *The composing processes of twelfth graders*. Urbana IL: NCTE.

Escoffier, J. (1990, Fall). Inside the ivory closet. *Outlook*, 40–48.

Flower, L., and Hayes, J. R. (1988). The cognition of discovery: Defining a rhetorical problem. In Tate, G., and Corbett, E. P. J. (Eds.), *The writing teacher's sourcebook* (2nd Ed.) (pp. 92–102). New York: Oxford University Press.

Freire, P. (1970). *Pedagogy of the oppressed*. (M. B. Ramos, Trans.). New York: Seabury Press.

Freire, P., and Macedo, D. (1987). *Literacy: Reading the word and the world*. South Hadley, MA: Bergin & Garvey.

Gilligan, C. (1982). *In a different voice*. Cambridge, MA: Harvard University Press.

Goleman, D. (1990, July 10). Homophobia: Scientists find clues to its roots. *The New York Times*, pp. C1, C11.

Hall Carpenter Archives Lesbian Oral History Group. (1989). *Inventing ourselves: Lesbian life stories*. London: Routledge.

Halliday, M. A. K. (1978). *Language as social semiotic*. London: Edward Arnold.

Hart, E. L. (1988). Literacy and the lesbian/gay learner. In Parmeter, S. H., and Reti, I. (Eds.), *The lesbian in front of the classroom: Writings by lesbian teachers* (pp. 30–43). Santa Cruz, CA: HerBooks.

Heath, S. B. (1983). *Ways with words*. New York: Cambridge University Press.

Macrorie, K. (1984). To be read. In Graves, R. L. (Ed.), *Rhetoric and composition: A sourcebook for teachers and writers* (pp. 81–88). Portsmouth, NH: Boynton/Cook. (Reprinted from English Journal 57, May 1968, pp. 686–692).

Milgram, S. (1990). The perils of obedience. In Hunt, D. (Ed.), *The dolphin reader*. (2nd Ed.) (pp. 431–444). Boston: Houghton Mifflin. (Reprinted excerpt from Milgram, S., *Obedience to Authority* (1974). New York: Harper and Row.)

Moffett, J. (1982). Writing, inner speech, and meditation. *College English 44,* pp. 231–244.

Mohr, R. D. (1988). *Gays/justice: A study of ethics, society, and law.* New York: Columbia University Press.

New York City Gay/Lesbian Anti-Violence Project. (1990). *Stop the violence.* (Informational leaflet distributed at the March Against Lesbian and Gay Violence, June 1990.) New York: Author.

Patton, C. (1990). *Inventing AIDS.* New York: Routledge.

Perl, S. (1988). Understanding composing. In Tate, G., and Corbett, E. P. J. (Eds.), *The writing teacher's sourcebook* (2nd Ed.) (pp. 113–118). New York: Oxford University Press. (Reprinted from *College Composition and Communication* (1980 *31,* 363–69)

Rose, M. (1989). *Lives on the boundary.* New York: Penguin.

——— (1990). This wooden shack place: The logic of an unconventional reading. *College English 41,* 287–298.

Seabrook, J. (December, 1990). The AIDS philosopher. *Vanity Fair,* 94–111.

Sedgwick, E. K. (1990). *Epistemology of the closet.* Berkeley CA: University of California Press.

Shor, I. (1980). *Critical teaching and everyday life.* Boston: South End Press.

——— (Ed.) (1987). *Freire for the classroom: A sourcebook for liberatory teaching.* Portsmouth, NH: Boynton/Cook.

Tracey, L. (1990, September 12). School gayze. *Outweek,* 85–86.

Part Four

RESTRUC-TURING TEACHER EDUCATION

I now realize that my supervisor was actually arguing for a revolution — that the lower orders be the ones whose every word really *mattered*, whose meaning be upheld as interesting. We had to change our use of the very word "interesting": no longer were we to appropriate it for ourselves.

— *Robert Coles*

The Conse-quences of Restructuring Teacher Education

*Robert J. Beichner and
James L. Collins*
State University of New York at Buffalo

Susan Szymanski
Heim Middle School, Williamsville, New York

*E*leven teachers and two professors wait on the sidewalk in front of O'Brien Hall, home of the University at Buffalo's Law School. They talk in pairs and groups, and the talk is mostly about what they have in common, their work teaching writing and science to sixteen children. A faded and dented blue van pulls up and kids climb out, early ones animatedly and then others with seeming reluctance. The teachers and students greet each other, talk briefly, and in some cases look over the notebooks and maps they're all carrying. Then they walk away from the Law School and past the Graduate School of Education. They go by Lockwood Library and take a shortcut through Alumni Arena, the physical education building. A half mile later they're in the woods.

In this chapter we tell the story of these teachers and kids and their work in a graduate teacher-education course called "Writing to Learn

Science." We briefly describe what was done in the course, but our real purpose is to share what we learned about the consequences of restructuring. Throughout the chapter we include excerpts from co-author Susan Symanski's journal, written while she was a teacher enrolled in the course, to illustrate connections among educational structures, teaching, and learning.

"Writing to Learn Science" was from the outset an experiment in restructuring teacher education. Instead of the usual trappings — lectures and textbooks to tell teachers what to do, demonstrations and microteachings to simulate teaching, cases and discussions to examine teaching — the course took direct teaching experience to be the foundation of teacher education. It combined a graduate seminar for teachers with a science class for middle school students, and for teachers and students alike the main idea was to learn from experience and from reflecting on experience. Teachers in the seminar worked each day with the science students and then discussed their work with one another after the students had gone home, aiming to understand and improve their teaching. The course avoided the usual boundaries isolating classrooms, grades, ability levels, and content areas, and it especially avoided the boundary separating teachers and students. Teachers enrolled in the course were middle school and high school English and science teachers, and each teacher formed a working team, or partnership, with one or two children. The children were Native Americans, seventh- and eighth-graders, who had been described as "kids unmotivated by science." The course used computers to combine writing and science, but mostly this was field-based teacher education — with the field consisting of forest, clearings, wildlife, and a paved recreation trail adjacent to a wide, meandering creek bordering the University at Buffalo campus.

Planning New Structures

Our intentions for the class were twofold. We wanted to have preservice and practicing teachers explore ways they might use writing in their teaching, and we wanted to help the seventh- and eighth-graders realize that science can be fun and that they might be able to pursue it on their own. We planned science activities in which we had teachers and kids participate in the discovery, observation, and classification of data. And we planned writing activities to help the teachers and kids transform their experiences of discovery, observation, and classification into knowledge. Thus, we conceived of writing-to-learn science in a broad and open sense; for both teachers and students, we wanted writing to serve learning as a means of making sense of experience.

The teachers' writing took the form of double-entry journals. Teachers divided each page of their notebooks vertically in half and kept a record of their work in a "Performance" column on the left-hand side. They later added thoughts about their work in a "Reflections" column on the right-hand side of the page. Here is an excerpt from Susan's initial journal entry, composed on the first day the course met. In this excerpt, "we" refers only to teachers, since the students joined us for the first time on the following day:

6/28 Today we went over what we'll be doing in the course. We'll alternate going outside to learn about science with writing about what we have learned. The messages we want to convey to the kids:

1. This is interesting and fun.
2. People do these things for real.
3. Kids can produce knowledge.
4. If you are interested in the world, then you are a scientist already.

We also wrote in response to some questions:

1. What is science?
2. Describe a typical scientist's day.
3. Could you be a scientist?

I think the kids will enjoy going out and exploring the woods. And I know I will, too. Kids often hate science (and writing, for that matter) because teachers have taken the fun and ownership out of learning.

In reflecting on the science questions, I realized how little I know about science. My teachers didn't make it fun—it was just confusing memorization. How important it is for us teachers to learn that we are paid to teach and help kids learn, not just to present material for kids to memorize.

The students' writing also combined observations and reflections, but not in the form of double-entry journals. While observing in the woods, students took notes in plastic-covered notebooks we provided. Later, back in the classroom, they wrote about their observations by transforming their notes into reports, as in this example from one of them:

First Day at UB

The first day I got to UB, there were many different things to experience.

The first thing we saw was some weeds. They looked like they were pushed over but we found out that the weeds had been cut down by someone. We thought the reason the weeds were cut down was for parking spaces.

Further on we came to some water. We looked at it and it had something that looked like slime in it. When we started walking away there was a dog named Heidi that went down to the water. She sniffed the water and left. She sensed that the water wasn't good to drink.

When we first got on the bike trail we saw some ducks. There was about seven of them. There were ducking their heads under the water, it looked like they were looking for food. A couple of them walked up on land toward us.

The water looked better then the water Heidi was sniffing but it had different shades of colors. It had brown, dark brown, green and dark green. We think that what caused the different shades was pollution and/or moss.

We then went down to the Creek and saw bubbles coming up from the water. There were soft floressent pinkish spots in the water. I picked up a stick from the water and it looked like it had oil all over it. The water smelled gross!

When we got back on the trail we saw some mile markers. We marked them in our notes so that we could make a map. We counted our steps between the mile markers.

Learning Activities

We organized the activities of the course into four major tasks. The first was a mapmaking project, consisting of mapping the wooded area and locating its major physical and biological features. Second, a professor who had studied the more than 200 varieties of trees on our campus conducted an exercise in identifying and studying trees in the wooded area. Third, another professor who systematically studies birds on and around our campus organized a task that involved locating and identifying birds in the area. Finally, an engineer from the Army Corps of Engineers led the teachers and students in studying the flood-control function of the area by explaining a just-completed project to prevent the creek in the wooded area from flooding nearby residential neighborhoods.

For the mapmaking exercise, the initial one we used with the kids, we obtained a map of the wooded area from the town engineers. We deleted the two-mile paved recreation trail from the map. We gave each teacher-student team a copy of the incomplete map and asked them to go into the wooded area, chart the course of the creek, and locate the trail accurately on their maps; we also suggested they take note of other features worth mapping in the study area, and we asked them to take notes on the mapping experience so they could write about it the next day.

Our "tree expert" accompanied us on one of the walks and told the students, mostly through brief lectures, about selected trees in the wooded area. After his presentation, the students made leaf rubbings and wrote descriptions of their leaves to share with other groups. It became sort of a detective game. One group wrote as careful a description of a leaf as they could and another group would take those paragraphs and try to identify the tree from a guidebook. They also wrote down their own steps to take in identifying a tree; in effect, they made their own guidebooks.

Our "bird expert" sent the student and teacher teams into the woods to observe birds and take notes on their characteristics. They carefully recorded what they considered to be important facts in their notebooks, and for most of them this turned out to be the favorite activity of the entire semester: sitting quietly in the woods, waiting for birds, recording as much detail as possible before a bird flew away. Back in the classroom after observing birds in the field, they used several bird guidebooks and their field notes to determine what kinds of birds they had seen. We then gave the students short descriptions of twenty local birds. They used these paragraphs and their notes to make their own bird guidebooks.

The flood-control engineer showed us the work of the Army Corps of Engineers and explained, again mostly by lecturing, how the system of gates and culverts was planned and built. He talked at much greater length than the other visitors and, probably as a result, inspired much less writing on his topic than the others did on theirs.

Restructuring Writing and Learning

What we learned from our experiment in restructuring teacher education is that educational practice reflects educational structure. The innovative structure of "Writing to Learn Science" altered the ways we thought about writing and science.

As the teachers and kids teamed up and went about making sense of their experiences in the environment we studied, they used writing in support of their work, but they didn't do so in only the one way predicted by our planning, i.e., by transforming notes into reports. We now realize that even though we had designed a very nontraditional teacher-education course, we had throughout our planning held a rather traditional notion of school writing, a notion built on the lingering assumption that producing accepted forms of academic writing matters more than other functions of writing. Perhaps the major consequences of restructuring "Writing to Learn Science" was the realization that an academic essay by itself is not much better than the standard lab report found in so many science classes. Both emphasize packaging knowledge, rather than generating or discovering it.

Teachers followed our advice to model the writing process for their students, but otherwise ideas of what constitutes writing and how writing can serve learning changed substantially during the course of the semester. We had originally planned to have the children take field notes on their observations, write interim narrative reports based on the notes, and then collect the reports in a "science book" written by the students. The course syllabus stated, "If this group project is thorough enough, it will be 'real science' in the sense that no one else has studied the area's biology as carefully." This planned writing, however, proved inconsistent with the structure of our course. The kids and their teachers seemed too busy working together and generating knowledge from observations, knowledge about one another and about the environment we studied, to do "regular" school writing, especially since some of the students weren't very good at such writing. Susan's journal mentions reluctance to write and also suggests how a writing partner might help:

7/12 My partner's name is Stacy. He is 13 and going into 7th grade. At first I thought he was going to be quiet and shy, but he opened up and was quite friendly and relaxed. When we did the interest inventory, I asked him questions and wrote down things about him and then asked him to do the same for me. He did not mind asking the I would guess that he has very little experience with writing. He has probably not yet experienced much (if any) success with writing. He was very quick to respond that he doesn't like writing.

questions, but he didn't seem to enjoy the writing.

Stacy is observant but not thrilled about writing down our observations. He did so with encouragement. I think he will be reluctant to write, but [my] modeling and encouragement will help.

I was absolutely *thrilled* with the enthusiasm of Stacy, Jeremiah, and Doug when we took the walk. They were very observant and very interested. I am impressed with their knowledge of the outside world.

Function follows structure, and the mapmaking project provides a good example of how teachers' understanding of the functions of writing, and the students' degree of writing reluctance, changed. While exploring the wooded area, everyone took notes and made sketches for use in mapmaking. And when they returned to the classroom, students and their teacher-partners took a great interest in transforming their notes and recollections into poster-sized, multicolored maps, as in the case of Susan and Stacy:

7/14 The mapping was fun. The more details we put on the map, the more interesting the activity became. It's hard to determine how much to do and how much to have the kids do. I wrote on the map, but always with Stacy's input. I think it made him more comfortable, but I know he will only be interested as long as he is actively involved.

I am impressed with the students' knowledge of the outside world. Who said these kids didn't like science? They certainly like this kind of science. Of course, not all students will always enjoy everything, but if the majority of students dislike a certain subject, then something is wrong, and it is the teacher's responsibility to do something to change kids' attitude about the program. Exploring, observing, and recording the past couple days has taught me that learning science *is* fun — not at all the way I found it as a student in school.

The three boys I walked with most of the time seemed to know quite a bit about science — outdoor life science. They didn't know things in a textbook-like way, and they didn't know scientific terms.

The more kids enjoy learning, the more they will learn. I am repeating this point because I feel it is one of the most valuable things to be learned in this experience.

The course plan had hoped the mapping project would lead to writing, but why write about making a map when you can make one? And doesn't doing something provide at least as much learning, and a good deal more enjoyment, as writing about doing it? These were the points students and teachers seemed to be arguing through their busy pleasure with the mapping project. As for writing-to-learn, there is very little real difference between writing sentences and paragraphs and putting words and symbols on a map. Both are intellectual activities involving the rendering of reality in symbols. Both involve planning, recording, and revising, and both contribute to good science. Even the students who did write about mapmaking placed less emphasis on writing than on creating knowledge; the recording of data seemed to take on primary importance to them, as in the case of one girl who wrote in a narrative, "We took good notes so that we could make a map the next day and write this story!"

Writing-to-learn can take the form of field notes, words and symbols on a map, or any other form that helps accomplish the work of learning. In fact, careful notes during field experiences seemed to be the most valuable kind of writing to our students. When reluctant writers come to value writing for its function, writing teachers have done their jobs well.

Restructuring Participation

The mapmaking project also illustrates the point that in writing-to-learn, and probably in most other aspects of schooling, the person who does the work does the learning. The teacher-student teams allowed kids, with assistance from adult partners, to control the structure of their own learning and become active learners. As one teacher put the matter in his journal, "The reason I think it went so well was because the kids had gathered all the information themselves and therefore they cared about the accuracy of the map. They had a personal invest-ment in the project—it was their own discoveries and observations, and they wanted to record them properly."

Other activities in "Writing to Learn Science" support the notion of control of structure as a key to active learning. During the second major activity, the tree-identification project, the students had been quite bored while outside listening to the brief lectures about trees, except when a deer appeared in the woods and watched the kids for what seemed like a long time before bounding away. What makes a lecture boring is not the classroom, or the length of the lecture, or sitting still in an uncomfortable chair. Our visiting professor's lectures were brief, less than five minutes on each of the trees he described for us, and the kids were in the woods, sitting on the ground. The lectures were boring to our seventh- and eighth-graders because the professor was doing all the work of making sense of the environment; the kids were limited to listening and watching him do it. When they were inside the next day, producing leaf rubbings and writing descriptions of leaves, the boredom disappeared and students were highly motivated to describe and identify trees. They produced their own guidebooks and also wrote "detective game" descriptions to trade with other students.

7/19 Today we met the plant and tree expert, and he guided us through a walk along the bike path where we identified different types of trees by their leaves, bark, and shape. He had a handout that pictured the different types of leaves and trees and he explained everything very clearly, but the kids were only somewhat interested. They kept darting off to look for discoveries of their own. They just didn't seem too much to want to listen.

Stacy was pretty much like I've described the majority of the group, kind of disinterested. He didn't seem to want to talk much, and he only wrote in his notebook a few times.

I learned a lot from this experience. The kids could not keep interested because they were not actively involved. We had given them a taste of freedom and independent exploration and they didn't want us to take that away. The point is, I guess, that as a teacher it is not so much that you are super well prepared (the professor was) as it is that you have developed lessons and activities where the students are active and interested. Kids want to learn inductively—discover and observe, and when interest and activity peak, let's figure out what we know. The session was scheduled like regular school—teacher gives info and students listen. The kids were just not thrilled about this, especially after we had already let them learn actively and inductively.

I think the experience could have been more successful if we had let the kids go out into the woods and discover for themselves how leaves and trees are different and develop a method for identifying them, and then go back in the classroom and figure out the identification process and clarify what we have learned.

The bird-identifying part of the course presented a direct contrast to the tree-identifying project. This time the visiting professor sent student-teacher teams and partners off on their own. He told them to sit as still and quiet as possible in a part of the woods of their choosing, recording in their notebooks as much information as possible about birds they see. The next day they had to identify the birds they had seen by matching their notes with pictures and written descriptions provided by the professor. Susan's prediction at the end of the above journal entry comes true in the next one:

7/26 What a successful day. We paired up with Lisa and Jeremiah to look for birds and record our observations about them. Jeremiah and Stacy really enjoyed the challenge of finding birds and recording as much information about them as they could. I was so pleased, not only with their enthusiasm for exploration, but also by their willingness to record in writing what they observed. I think they both really wanted to be able to identify the birds correctly on Friday and they knew they would need accurate notes to do so.

What an effective way of teaching the importance and value of writing: make it personally meaningful. Although that is not what I originally thought was meant by "writing" in this course, that is truly *writing-to-learn*. They knew they needed to write to accomplish their goal, and so they did. It clarifies for me that writing-to-learn does not mean copying passages of a textbook so you remember them. It means recording meaningful information (in various forms) for a particular purpose. It doesn't always require complete sentences and paragraphs, but it is writing, purposeful writing. I like the fact that we (the teachers) did not have the answers. We were co-learners and in a natural, meaningful way we shared our learning processes. We worked together, all of us on the same level. I think it was very effective.

Writing Partnership

Restructuring teacher education to form partnerships with students led to co-authoring as a way of teaching and learning writing. We want to clarify what we mean by "co-authoring" by saying a little about the pedagogical approach used by teachers in "Writing to Learn Science" to help students with writing. The approach is called "Writing Partnership," and it's built on the idea that writing partners do more than teach, consult, or confer with writers. Through collaboration writing partners show how successful writers work, and they show what successful writing looks like. The idea of writers working in collaboration is certainly not new, but for reluctant writers accustomed to struggling with literacy in isolation, partnership can be a refreshing and profitable approach.

Writing partnership means collaboration in the fullest sense of the word, in the sense of sharing the work of writing. In a writing partnership one writer helps another by taking over some of the work to demonstrate or exemplify how a writer goes about writing. A writing partner, for example, might help a writer turn a sentence into a paragraph by asking for specifics and writing them down, much as a woodworking teacher might help a student by running the first board through the table saw to show the student how it's done.

Writing partnerships can obviously be useful with problems of syntax, mechanics, and spelling. Here the writing partner can provide varying degrees of help: a list of problems to be worked on, a thorough discussion of only one problem, or a sample of how to go about finding and eliminating all occurrences of one type of error. Another obvious occasion for help from a writing partner is when writing has an inappropriate expressive character, such as when it resembles unedited verbal thought. In the following example, a teacher helped two writers transform their first draft into more explicit writing by questioning them for more information on content and organization and by helping them to type the information into the computer:

Initial Draft:

> yesterday we saw mallard ducks and two baby ducks. then we saw a snake and becky didn't throw it in to see if it was a water snake. we followed deer tracks then we cornered a deer and it almost hit leif. then it went through the field. and then we seen the red tailed hawks by the radio tower. then at the bridge jeremy caught a grandpa crayfish.

Final Draft:

> **Summer Observations**
> *by Leif Twoguns and Les Parry*
> This is going to be about tracking and finding and observing birds, fish and animals in the area of U.B. we studied this summer.

We'll start with deer. The first sign of deer we noticed was tracks in the mud. You can tell deer tracks by their pattern of two half circles separated at the front of the track. They look like two half moons. The best place to look for these tracks is in the woods and where it's muddy, like on the bank of the creek. The way to spot a deer in the woods is by its brownish tan color and by its eyes looking at you. As long as you stand still, the deer will watch you and not move. It must figure you can't see it as long as it is standing still.

Now we'll talk about crayfish. A crayfish looks like a little lobster. There are two claws, eight legs and two antennae. The crayfish can be brown, green, black or a very light tan color. You find them by going to a creek or stream with very little rapids. You turn over rocks, being very watchful because otherwise the crayfish might pinch you with its claws. When you find one, you can pick it up by either scooping it up with both hands or by lifting it with two fingers in the middle of its back. You cut off the tail, and then you can eat the crayfish; you can either boil it or eat it raw. It almost tastes like crab.

Finally, we'll end with red-tailed hawks. The size of a red-tailed hawk is usually about the same as a crow. Some of the tail feathers are red, brown and white, which is what gives the bird its name. The beak is pointed and hooked and is used to tear the meat when the bird is dining on its prey. The hawks eat fish, snakes and mice. When they locate their prey, they soar in a circle and dive for it when the prey is in just the right spot. The head of the hawk and the feathers are used for Indian outfits for ceremonial purposes.

Indians use Red Tailed Hawk or Bald Eagle feathers for their dance (powwows), traditional dancing for entertainment. They have contests at different places like the Erie County Fair. We get money for dancing! Lots of people watch the dances. There are three types of outfits. Traditional, grass, and fancy. The traditional outfit is like the old type of dancing, the way Indians used to dance a long time ago, with feathers moving around. Grass dancing is like the wind blows the grass. Fancy is the new kind of dancing. It is really fast. The outfits are colorful, all made out of feathers. The grass outfits are made out of yarn. Leif's two little brothers have traditional outfits. Leif has a grass outfit which was made by his mother.

Other Consequences of Restructuring

Not everything we learned from our experiment in restructuring teacher education was learned in a clear, positive, and well-defined way, and we want to close this chapter with a look at a couple of the less settled observations we made. Our intention is not to undermine what we've already said; we definitely believe restructuring in the direction of learner participation and control is good for education. Still, not everyone was comfortable with every aspect of our course, and we want to point out some of the sources of discomfort.

Most teachers in the course appreciated working within the equitable student-teacher relationships we established, but some didn't. The teachers were learning science facts along with their student partners, and this caused some anxiety. "Learning science through discovery is wonderful, but I feel very uncomfortable discovering along with the students. At first I thought it was the feeling of insecurity that bothered me. However after much reflection I realize that this type of experience does not allow for as enriching an experience for the student as it might have been if I had been afforded the opportunity to learn and plan before taking the students out on the trail . . . as a professional, I feel it is my responsibility to know as much about a subject as possible before introducing it in the classroom." We spent a good deal of time discussing this issue, and even so, the discomfort some teachers felt about giving up some authority never really went away.

We also learned that getting to know students is not always easy, especially when cross-cultural factors are involved, and we learned anew that kids often have different values from adults. Kids are kids, capable of surprises, annoyances, and occasional cruelties. Giving up some teacher authority and control and working in close partnership with them shouldn't mean not stepping in when it's felt that clear and decisive direction is needed. Susan's journal speaks to this point:

7/26 I observed something today that bothered me. One group of boys found a large crayfish in the creek and kept it. Later I found out that on the walk to the bus, they smashed it against a wall and left it to die. I'm not overly sentimental about the death of one crayfish, but I am concerned that we allowed that treatment of a living creature of nature on our class time under our supervision.

I'm not sure I understand the kids in terms of their culture; the way they interact with nature puzzles me. I expected them to exhibit a reverence and respect for nature, and they did not. That brings me to one more thought about the crayfish incident. I don't think it is our place to indoctrinate kids with what we feel is right or wrong with how we treat our natural world. Certainly we are not going to change too many opinions and practices in one course. I do feel, however, that we had the perfect opportunity to say something about respecting nature and that when we explore, we observe but do not destroy, and we passed up that opportunity. I think it was part of our responsibility as teachers taking kids out to learn about nature.

Still, most of the consequences of restructuring teacher education through "Writing to Learn Science" were positive, even the unintended consequences. The course generated considerable reflection on what it means to be a teacher and how that relates to interaction with students. Everyone—teacher and student alike—was involved in observing, recording, and learning. The student-teacher partnerships represented cooperative learning at its best. Teachers and students teamed up to solve the problems we presented, and adjusting the ratio of student-teacher talk in favor of greater responsibility for kids called out increased performance from them. The partnerships also made learning a two-way street. Some of the boys, for example, taught their teachers how to interpret holes in the ground—which holes were made by animals and which holes are still occupied: "Those holes are from mice, but they haven't been used for a while. Animals keep their doors clear of leaves and dirt."

The course met its parallel objectives of helping teachers to improve their teaching and bringing students to a better understanding of the nature of science and the science in nature. By restructuring the course we reformulated what we meant by writing, teaching, and learning and thus confirmed our suspicion that the function of teacher education follows from its structure.

Teachers Talk About Restructuring: A Conversation in Fifteen Voices

Sally Hudson-Ross
University of Georgia
and the English teachers of Rockdale County, Georgia

*E*veryone else is at school on this blustery October Wednesday, and we feel a lot like kids skipping out. In our most comfortable sweats, we sprawl across Liz's living room furiously writing letters. Some write while on their tummies on the floor, others curl up in corners of chairs and couches, all try in thirty minutes to describe for each other how our classrooms have changed and what a difference these changes have made for us.

We worked together in August 1990, fourteen very traditional high school English teachers and I, and we have come together again to reflect on our experiences in our own classrooms and on our efforts to bring the theory and practice of Nancie Atwell's *In the Middle* (1987) into the high school setting. In the sharing of our letters, we will come to realize almost reverently how far we have come. Jo volunteers to begin the conversation. We invite you to listen.

Jo Gault, teacher of ninth grade, October 1990

You know I was one of "those" people last year who didn't know what integrated language was. I had little instruction, but after visiting a middle school, I liked what I saw and dabbled in it, picking and choosing those things that I liked.

Then came Summer! I was not at all sure this old dog could learn so many new tricks. It was not an easy task to go into this "whole hog," but I decided I would try.

I began my year using a background of the eight parts of speech, the five stages of the nouns and pronouns, the four types of sentence construction, and the three kinds of dependent clauses. We studied this for just a week, but from then on we used it as a reference point.

The next step was setting up the writing and reading workshops. We just started to write. We brainstormed, had peer conferences and teacher conferences. The students wrote with very little prodding. On the reading days, I would read something to them for them to "freewrite" about or we would write literary letters to friends about the books we were reading. Then we would read in our pleasure books. Some students have read one book, and some students have read ten books since August, but they are reading with some enjoyment.

I have introduced the required grammar by putting the learning on their shoulders. The book has a diagnostic test at the beginning. They do this at home, and we check it in class. Then I assign the chapter to be read, and the review and mastery tests to be completed at home. We check these in class, and each student makes out a skill sheet. Any error is placed on the skill sheet. They are to study the notes that I give in class and the other exercises in the book as needed. I then test them over the chapter, having spent very little time in class on this. After the test, they go back to the skill sheet and record anything they are still having problems with.

I'm using the Short Story Unit as a co-op group. There are three groups, and each group is responsible for reading all twenty-one stories. *They* divide them between the group members, and each Wednesday, three or four students discuss a story that was assigned to them. I don't know the outcome yet.

I'm convinced this is the way to go. The students are interested and interesting. They participate, they question, they help, and the class is pleasant. They're amazingly good at helping those who were absent or new students who need to understand our structure. We even look forward to each class.

How about this! This old dog has learned new tricks, and she loves it!

* * *

"Bravo!" we cheer. And Lorraine follows excitedly.

Lorraine Fussell, teacher of ninth grade, all levels, and one tenth-grade basic, October 1990

Most of my success in this about-face proposition has come from our reading workshops. Since I have the dubious honor of teaching many of the same students as both ninth- and tenth-graders, I can monitor their progress in ways that most other teachers can't. Last year most of my ninth-grade Coordinated Vocational and Academic Education (CVAE) students equated reading with dental procedure and other intrusive, painful operations, although I did allow them, even then, personal choice in reading.

The use of whole language techniques, however, has transformed some of these same reluctant readers into avid ones—ones who beg me to have reading days. I can think of one student in particular who didn't read a single full-length book last year. This year he reads constantly. He came back to class one day, thrilled that he'd finished a Louis L'Amour western within a week. He was ready to find another book the minute he walked into class.

Our classroom library has grown quite large, and I've begun to feel like a teacher-librarian now that a significant portion of time between classes is devoted to checking books in and out. But I'm not complaining. One of the greatest joys I've ever had as a teacher has been witnessing these miraculous transformations.

* * *

Jo's and Lorraine's students are becoming readers and writers, far more than ever before. No, the curriculum hasn't been dropped, but it has been pushed aside just far enough and just long enough to allow teachers to find their own comfort zones and students to find room to grow. And the kids are emerging, full-spirited and in charge. We begin to realize that once the conversion to a student-centered classroom is made, the students themselves will allow no going back.

Liz Brinkley, teacher of tenth-grade basic and gifted classes and twelfth-grade advanced placement, October 1990

The students cheered when they heard the idea of a writing/reading workshop. And that "puzzled" me. I was so excited at first but somewhat insecure. All started well. I taught in mini-lessons. Status of Class Report was a great war, to keep track, but it was going, and they were reading, and they were writing.

One boy wrote that this class was like no other in the world! "And I love it," he added. One father came to find out what was going on and if students were really being taught to write. He left saying he'd drop in one day and write with us!

Then, it hit. The Basic Skills Test took a solid week away from two of my classes. Then an assembly hit some classes. I panicked! "I am behind," plagued my thoughts. I decided (here's my biggest learning experience) I would *take back* a week to catch up on *my* mini-lessons. I did so in spite of the moans and "you promised" comments.

The second day of *my* week I saw so clearly: students looking out the window, sleeping, discipline problems evolving. I reprimanded a girl for not knowing the page number. "I already know this stuff; I was trying to finish my poem," she said in a tone of "it's your fault." "Yea! This is boring," chimed in two or three others. "Let's just go back to *real* class. You can count off *bad* if we miss these pronouns!" said a boy who had been keeping up and participating.

"O.K." I gave in and said, "Get your folders."

And they cheered!

* * *

So do we! Can it really be working this well? There is far more here than "doing" journals or literary responses or conferencing. We agree it had been easy to add on layers of student discussion, group work, or motivational strategies after each wave of inservice over the years. But this is different. Shared ownership of our classrooms forces us to see beyond ourselves, and in new ways.

June Johnston, teacher of ninth-grade gifted English classes, October 1990

The most positive aspect that whole language has brought to my classroom is a change in my philosophy of teaching. And after twenty years or so, don't we all need a change once in a while! At this stage my philosophy is stronger (and thriving more) than my methods. I guess that can be both good and bad. I feel good about *myself* and what I am doing, but I don't always feel good about how I do it. I'm learning each day (perhaps I should say moment) what works and what doesn't. I just hope I won't be afraid to try my "failed" methods again with a different group of kids.

I'm experimenting more than ever with shifting responsibility from the teacher to the student. I have been in charge for so long (and I think rather enjoyed it), but it does make the job less stressful when I'm not accountable for everything and everybody. My students are struggling with accepting this accountability and even get mad when I won't do it or tell them that it doesn't matter.

The second most positive aspect is a shift from grading to learning. I was so ready to stop recording so much and just say something is OK—it's one person's best attempt *or* honest attempt, and I don't need to judge it by my established (or indoctrinated) standards. We have become more "suggestion makers" for one another, and it is such a fun way to write and discuss literature. Essays have several readers who make suggestions both good and bad, and the final grade tends to be less important. They're learning a lot from their "mess-ups." Letting students select best papers for final grades also helps alleviate that awful grade pressure.

I'm still struggling with a balance between this and my treasured traditional approach and hope I can bring the "best of both worlds" to my students. My gifted students generally don't need whole language as a motivational factor. They are motivated already. But they truly need whole language to broaden their narrow scope and see the excitement of new ideas, new approaches, and new standards. They need to be excited about language and literature as experience and process and not always a product.

I'm having fun watching and guiding them to become thinkers and process learners. I'm ready to throw away the grade book! All of mine are going to pass—no, all are doing very well because they are learning and thinking (and they are not always my thoughts—heaven forbid!!—that sounds like heresy, doesn't it?).

I still have a lot to learn! Help! I have problems too.

*   *   *

Of course we do. We all have problems. How to get kids to put more heart and depth into literary letters to one another? How to guide writing processes without taking over? How to keep up with 150 students, 30 at a time? How to deal with the limitations of school-wide tracking? But those are things we can deal with all afternoon. In the meantime, we sense that the bigger changes we are hearing about will make our conversations more purposeful. Struggling with technicalities, management, and lack of student commitment is one thing when they are issues of discipline and control; it is something quite different when they are issues of learning.

Scott Gordon, teacher of ninth- and tenth-grade basic students, October 1990

English is the first language of all the students I teach. Somewhere along the way, though, in the classroom, English has been taken away from the students, and, in their point of view, it has become some mysterious, indecipherable, unattainable language used by English teachers and other snobs. Whole language gives them their language back.

These students are succeeding because the teacher-imposed mystery of the language is gone. The student does not read a critic's or an editor's opinion; he simply reads for himself. The student doesn't read about writing; she writes. Simply put, the student is a critic and a writer.

I enjoy the class more because we operate more on a human level. We share, we help one another. We laugh at our mistakes, and we praise good work. The idea of a teacher existing to impart knowledge creates an artificial situation. In the whole-language classroom we are all students, and we are all teachers. This cooperation seems to reflect the "real world" much more.

*   *   *

Although we love what we were seeing and feeling so far, restructuring at this level isn't easy. None of us has ever experienced a school setting where such things go on, where students are invited into our spaces to learn together. Our students have certainly never experienced such things either. As we all experiment together, we all flounder; but when we don't fall back on illogical ways and irrational wisdom, trust builds a strong foundation for moving on. If we can just hang on that long.

Trish Thornton, teacher of English as a Second Language in two high schools, October 1990

Restructuring any classroom is a difficult task. It requires a willingness to tear down old structures that may be worm-eaten and ugly but secure. It means being willing to live in the midst of some disorder and the sounds of rebuilding for a while. It requires a vision of the new structure—a goal to be realized at a future time. Each new feature can be celebrated while the whole is in process, but the whole still seems unfinished and a bit insecure.

That's where my classes are right now. I can celebrate with my students in their enthusiasm for writing. *All* of them are trying harder and really seem to want to express themselves. But, we're still in process in the reading. They don't seem to find enjoyment in reading. It's a struggle. Their language skills are such that even materials designed for lower-level native speakers are a struggle. I'm wondering how to release them from the hands of that language problem. I'm trying a theme unit on "childhood" and that seems to be concrete enough to provide the structure they need.

The old structure is one of teacher-centered learning. The curriculum is predetermined and usually rigid. The new structure is student-centered and is determined as we go. To make that change is frightening. Although the teacher and students like it, it brings insecurity. Students sometimes fight it because it's easier not to have the control. They have to think and be responsible, and sometimes they don't know how. For the teacher, it's difficult not to step in and assume the control and responsibility. We are there to guide students, and sometimes we equate that with thinking for them.

The old structure also meant planning 50-minute lessons that seem orderly. There's a set agenda, and it seems more measurable. (I have a science background and measurable data is comfortable for me.) The new structure means letting students have an agenda.

* * *

Not only are teachers and students somewhat ill at ease, but there are other agendas—beyond the students'—that have to be met given the context of today's high school: administrative requirements for managing over a thousand people a day, parents' expectations, community traditions. We can't upend everything over night. Besides, we don't want to.

For example, we believe that a chronological approach in American and British literature gives students a sense of movements in literature and how history interacts with authors and literature of an era. We agreed back in August that a chronological unit could be introduced with two or three important and representative readings and mini-lessons for a week, but the next week or two, which might traditionally be spent "covering" everything else in the text on that period, could just as easily be devoted to free reading and sharing within this historical period. Writing workshops could alternate with reading workshops, and a final time for polishing, publishing, and celebrating could provide the review needed for the requisite semester exams. We don't have to throw out everything, just push back our agendas to make room for students to succeed.

Gayle Allen, teacher of eleventh grade, October 1990

In restructuring my classroom to use a whole-language approach to teaching eleventh-grade American literature following the curriculum restraints, I made compromises with whole-language philosophy. The major one is that I eliminated some of the choices by making some assignments in both reading and writing required. Another area where I bent the philosophy is that I set some deadlines for completed pieces and made me the evaluator of two of the pieces.

My class time is divided into two-week reading blocks followed by one-week writing blocks. Because of the open time at the end of the semester to finish projects, I was able to extend the second reading workshop to accommodate the projects that fourth and sixth period developed.

I made the decision that the class would take the individual research material to present in a whole-class project; the students chose the mode after brainstorming and discussing the advantages and disadvantages of each form. While some students were actually engaged in project work, the others continued reading until it was their group's turn.

The time in each class period is usually divided into an opening mini-lesson followed by a quick status-of-the-class report and reading or writing workshop. I either read or conference with the students during this time. I also use this time to respond to literary letters if we are in reading workshop.

A major advantage to my students in this program is that they are developing their insights into literature, not adapting mine. Another is that they are beginning to value their work a little more. An advantage to me is that I know my students and their abilities better.

*   *   *

Some teachers dramatically reshape Atwell's ideas for their high school settings. In Jerry Smith's class, the football captain has become enchanted by connections between Native American and football-team rites of passage and leadership roles and has actually enjoyed compiling and sharing an annotated bibliography on the subject. Required parent responses to student literary letters, which Jerry also invented, are powerful opportunities for family involvement and class sharing.

By midday I notice our interpretations of Atwell are no longer interpretations; they are simply *our* ways of teaching. And we hungrily share what we are doing with all the enthusiasm of beginners.

Jerry Smith, teacher of eleventh-grade American Literature and a humanities two-hour block covering both American literature and history, October 1990

I hear the murmur of hushed voices as I ascend to the podium and see stunned, aghast looks — the lectern comes down, and I sit on top of the table in place of the once revered lectern. What's happened? The traditional classroom is dead. — *ding dong*!

What's now occurring? Students are controlling their learning and inspiring this teacher to give them more — how? Simply, I must open new paths.

Exciting is an understatement, for students are exuberant and lively.

To begin, I set up a structure that provided a gradual progression to writing, yet a total bath in student-chosen reading. My class syllabus sets out which weeks will be more devoted to reading and which will be more devoted to writing. I found myself *slowly* starting the writing because I was petrified as to how to allow students to write, as opposed to making them write. Since the literature to be experienced is American literature, I give mini-lessons concerning history, genre, technique, fun author facts, etc. for the period being studied. Also, I suggest a group of readings from that particular period that students should read in order to fully experience the period, then we read in class for approximately forty minutes per day. Students respond *to* the literature in their logs, due at the end of the week, if not complete before. The logs should contain two letters to peers, one letter to me, and one letter to a parent. I read and respond. Points are given if the letters contain:

1. the mention of literature

2. the mention of the author
3. some form of opinion concerning the literary piece, author's style, whatever
4. depth to the writing
5. a response from the audience.

Points are awarded as all or nothing. Students themselves are responsible for getting adequate responses to their letters; they can pass them to a second person if the first doesn't have enough to say. The peer pressure builds. The success rate has been *incredible*.

Finally, there are group shares toward the end of the week. Also, students complete annotated bibliographies, following MLA style, based on historical and literary research conducted on each period of literature. They can read about anything related to the period in any way, but I encourage them to stay in one direction. These are shared enthusiastically through groups, class share, and bulletin boards of trivia we've picked up. We've learned that research is constantly an ah-ha experience.

Their grades will be higher this semester, and it's not because things are easier. They aren't being penalized for their weaknesses, they are working on them.

* * *

Other teachers find new ways to use tried and true activities and projects that have allowed students to share their understandings for years. However, differences in classroom conditions—choice, time, response, openness to student inquiry—lead to exciting differences in results.

Chris Cook, teacher of twelfth-grade British Literature, October 1990

I've learned many things, but the most impressive to me is how creative some of the students are. I'm even enjoying reading their essays more than watching my beloved football! By giving students options as to the type of project they do for each literature unit, I've seen some talents and some enthusiasm that do not surface in a teacher-controlled assignment. Some of these talents fall into a language-oriented ability. The creative writing (epics, romances, ballads) has amazed me with its honest-to-God outstanding quality. The oral presentations have revealed some truly effective public speakers. The musicians have written words and music and performed live in class; they have found musical scores entitled *Beowulf*; they have written music to go with ballads from the middle ages. The artists have done interpretations of scenes from *Beowulf*, pointillism reproductions of William Blake's Canterbury pilgrims, and watercolors of medieval castles. The construction-oriented students have built models of Anglo-Saxon mead halls and villages and torture devices of the middle ages (a bed of nails and a "stock").

I feel that one of my (previous) major weaknesses as a teacher has been cured by the reading workshop. It always bothered me that my students were not readers of anything except the literature book and assigned novels. Now, they read a book of their choice guided by my stipulation that it be an adventure novel or a nonfiction, etc. The one day a week of class that they are given to read this book has enabled students who thought they disliked reading to find that it was only the book they had read that they disliked. Yesterday, a boy complained that nonfiction was boring only to have his classmate say, "Ooh, you should read my book about these two murderers. And my boyfriend is reading about ..." Suddenly nonfiction had a new meaning!

* * *

And the conversation continues. Stretching for possibilities, finding new ways to use the resources around us, allowing students to learn and share, we explore where we were and where we might go—as we begin to allow learning, instead of always teaching directly.

LaVetta Scott, teacher of ninth and tenth grades, October 1990

I'm requiring less reading and allowing more choices. More reading as a whole is done due to this choice. It's fascinating how the true interests of kids come out.

The students have accepted the responsibility and are becoming independence-oriented. Some do not do well with less structure. Some cannot handle openness at first. It does take a while for most students to fall into a routine that is not as structured. I still have to stay on top of some students (e.g. in lit. logs) because they may/may not cover/meet requirements, but I'm realizing that learned behavior comes from daily practice. And they're doing better all the time.

My classroom has more movement, more socializing, but also more fun at work. We're doing more project/long-term work (to cover concepts) and all work is more student-focused. I've learned that students can/will do creative things if given the opportunity. I'm spending far less time in teaching and giving more time to students. And most important, students themselves feel as if they are discovering something about themselves.

Nancy Goss, teacher of tenth grade, October 1990

Students in a whole language program obviously have more freedom than their peers in a more structured classroom. I have found that there are both advantages and disadvantages to this. As far as the physical structure of the classroom is concerned, I have found that I cannot be overly picky about where they peer-conference. A number of students will conference right at their desk with a neighbor.

I've found also that it is advantageous to allow students to choose their own writing topics. In my average classes, a number of students chose to write poetry. I had ten or twelve poems in several writing folders. I have encouraged them to write other things besides poems, but I feel the one thing that has worked best is telling them that in their permanent writing folder by the end of the quarter they must have four graded pieces of writing and only one poem may be used. I also have a marvelous kit called *Openers For English Classes* by Ana Bourman. It's full of all kinds of goodies on cards that suggest ways to start English classes. There are several cards called "five-minute writing ideas" that suggest topics many students can spend thirty minutes writing on. Also there is a set of cards in the kit called "Famous Quotations." On each card there is a quotation by a famous person. Students are asked to respond to the quote. Many of the average kids appreciate these prompts.

I've learned that advanced students need no prodding when it comes to writing; average and basic do, however. While you can allow advanced students freedom of choice, others need a little more guidance.

I've also learned that requiring five literary letters a week may be too much for literature logs. Next quarter I'm cutting back to two or three. I'm going to be working more with responses they make to letters they write. A number of students write *very brief* responses to the letters they receive.

Students have told me that they don't like having three writing days, so I might restructure the number of writing and reading days I have. I found that in the past if I required five literature letters, some students used one of their writing or reading days to write literature letters.

Joyce Deskins, half-day teacher of ninth grade, October 1990

I appreciate any concept that piques the student's interest. The integrated English approach is an excellent provision to stimulate learning because it allows for individual differences by permitting freedom of choice of reading and writing material. In my English classes, including the basic one, I give students the opportunity to teach the mini-lessons. For example, during the short-story unit, I modeled the teaching of plot as related to Roald Dahl's "Poison." Next, we divided into four groups per class to study in depth setting, theme, point of view, and irony. Each group had free choice of a story that best suited the needs within the topic. Each group determined its own teaching methods such as lecture supplemented with listening to tapes, reading orally, preparing a puppet show, reenacting scenes, and free reading.

The most innovative approach was the use of a puppet show to demonstrate theme in "The Scarlet Ibis." For a backdrop, the students drew on the blackboard a dimensional drawing of the interior of a living room complete with fireplace, braided rug, sofa, furniture, lamps, overhead light, and wall hangings.

The enthusiasm generated by the students pleases me. I have been privileged to observe these young people practicing research, reading, writing, speaking, and group-interaction skills that will serve them well in the future.

JoAnn Witherington, teacher of eleventh grade American Literature, October 1990

One of the most astonishing results in using the whole-language approach is the positive response of the students (most of them, anyway). They love being able to choose their reading selections, even when I impose certain limitations. I've learned that they can gain insight and understanding about literary history and eras through independent reading, as long as there is ample time for discussion and response. For the first time I feel as if all my American literature students really understand Romanticism and its influence on writing of this time period.

Truly self-motivated students really grow in this approach. They enjoy and use every class minute well. I've had some students use some days to both write and read, especially when a particular selection gave them an idea for writing. Several nonreaders picked up an interest in reading. I think that's great. By the same token, I have students who have developed an intense desire to write. I've gotten poems from students who I would never have expected would write poetry. I have a student who is working on an adventure tale, and he is so excited he wants to share his successes every day.

These successes show me that this approach will work and students will learn. I also am learning and plan to change as change becomes necessary.

*   *   *

I think it's our students' successes that most intrigue us all day. No matter how we may adapt or change our strategies in the coming months, we're hooked on those cheers, we're addicted to their enthusiasm for learning and for life. We discuss the fact that growth is a process of continual rebuilding. If groups such as ours—formal or informal—come together to plan, to dream, and to build, who knows where our visions may take us? It simply requires being able to see old structures, even the classic high school, through new eyes. I think Trish, again, said it best:

Trish Thornton, continued, October 1990

There are so many more things to say—so many good things tempered by hesitations and problems. But as I think about this idea of restructuring, I'm intrigued by an analogy that keeps floating through my mind. I recently visited an antique mall/flea market that was in a converted factory. Isn't that what we're doing? We're taking a factory that's obsolete, producing products that are no longer useful, and changing it into a useful place. Maybe it's an antique mall—full of treasures for everyone. Maybe it's a unique home with new structures, new forms for the living room, etc. I'd like to develop that analogy further. Can I communicate it to students?

*   *   *

Humble silence fills our conversation this October day as much as talk and good cheer. The potential to make a difference is really here, within our grasp. We now understand that it is as close as the voices of our students. We invite you too to pull up a chair and listen.

REFERENCES

Atwell, N. (1987). *In the middle: Writing, reading, and learning with adolescents*. Portsmouth, NH: Boynton/Cook.

In Teachers' Hands: Reading Our Teaching Texts

Ruth Vinz
Boise State University

Prologue

Over the last twenty-odd years, teacher effectiveness and teaching reform advocates, making recognizable the names and reputations of many Ernest Boyers, John Goodlads, and Madeline Hunters, have rarely served as imaginative sources for understanding the complexities of teachers' work. Rather, the bulk of the reform literature is technocratic and functionalist, assuming teaching to be a series of acontextualized procedures performed upon learners. It all sounds deceptively and alluringly appealing—these formulaic and reified dictums that prescribe what teachers and teaching ought to be.

Ironically, teachers are rendered voiceless in the cacophony of outsiders' reform slogans and recipes for improvement. How is it that we've allowed these portraits to represent teachers' work as devoid of life or lust, deadly dull and unimaginative when simplified into "mastery teaching," "4MAT," "democracy in education," and "time-on task"? In this press to prescribe students' and teachers' work together, I must pause to ask myself: Just what is in teachers' hands that is not jaded or neglected by those who usurp teachers' voices?

I'm feeling that we teachers have allowed ourselves to become imprisoned in a labyrinth of imposed reforms. With uncertainty, we wander through someone else's agendas, often picking and choosing the paths of least resistance. While the architects of this labyrinth (societal expectations and ills, historical precedents, NAEP, or educational researchers, to name a few in a lengthy litany) engage in vague and tedious talk, we can find ways to reclaim the voices we've abdicated. By looking at our work carefully, we might find the voice to speak out clearly and strongly, sharing the meanings we've constructed from our experiences in the classroom.

The acts of articulating these meanings may help us actualize who we are and what we are about. In some ways, I'm suggesting that we "read" our teaching histories in much the same way we read any text — to open a field of inquiry. If meaning becomes the product of our engagement with this teaching "text," we are cast in the role of questioner, critic, and creator of our teaching lives.

I am sensitive to the difficulty in doing this. While a journey through our teaching experiences might appear self-absorbed if not dilettante, it may also suggest that freedom comes from within and that those resources of mind and spirit that keep us searching have the potential to lead us to freedom.

To help me objectify this experience of reading the teaching text, I'd like to step back at an aesthetic distance and inquire into several representations of how I see myself as teacher of literature. Admittedly, this creates ostranenie, a deformity of sorts, as parts are separated from the whole. Yet, through the following representations of teacher as archeologist, anthropologist, artist, and reformer, each endowed with specific contexts and circumstances, I'd like to suggest these metaphoric ways of thinking about being a teacher as a framework that juxtaposes the ideology of teaching with the teacher's sense of self. As a beginning point in an articulated reintegration of teacher with discussions of reform in teaching, I'd suggest the journey, study, and appreciation of teaching and learning by teachers can serve to ground or expand the nature and nurture of reform.

Something more is happening, though. Following the notion I've suggested for reading our teaching texts, Derridean deconstruction might remind us that the text's importance is in what it *does not say* more than what it does say. The essence of the text I will create lies not in its capacity to represent teachers or their voices in a reform movement. Possibly, the text will bear a relationship to the dynamics of intellect and feeling through which you might interrogate the conditions and circumstances of your teaching text. With this in mind, the following is meant to help you read and reread yourselves and invite you to interrogate what your work is as teacher.

Teacher as Archeologist

In the graveyard scene when Hamlet cradles the skull of Yorick, looking in and through the remains of what once was a man who "hath borne me on his back a thousand times," I hear and see saliency in the artifacts of past human imaginings and actions. Literary texts are artifacts in a shared culture of what it means to be human. Through these we nudge students to unearth the shades of human folly and invention and to think through personal experiences as part of the larger culture and history.

"Alas, poor Yorick! I knew him, Horatio, a fellow of infinite jest, of most excellent fancy ... Where be your gibes now? Your gambols, your songs, your flashes of merriment, that were wont to set the table on a roar?" Yes, to unearth the bones, relics, rituals, and dust of our cultural imagination. The gibes are still there along with the gambols, songs, and merriments. Have we only to turn students on and into the words and visions that will lead them to themselves through their participation in the shared culture? It's not that simple.

In N. Scott Momaday's *The Ancient Child* (1989), I was struck by the following image of how the old woman, Koi-ehm-toya, seeing the children at play and outside her grasp or influence, agonizes at what will become of them:

> From the opening of her tipi, from the highest point in the camp, the old woman Koi-ehm-toya saw the children moving across the wrinkles of a meadow toward the trees. Zeid-le-bei! she thought; a bad business, dangerous. It was well past noon, and the light had begun to deepen. There were golden glints in the air and a faint haze on the woods. Koi-ehm-toya squinted and blinked her eyes, trying to see who the children were, but they were too far away, moving off, their backs to the camp. She counted them—five, six, seven—then counted them again. No, there were eight. Where did they think they were going? Were they being sent out to forage? That was not likely, after all. All the racks were hung with meat; no one was hungry. The children bobbed and skipped and tumbled away in the distance. Oh, they were only at play, she decided, running around and wasting their time, as children will do, giving not a thought to

their safety. She clicked her tongue and set a mask upon her face, a perfect scowl. And in the very way of an old woman she wondered aloud what was to become of the people, they had grown so careless. She scolded the children under her breath, but she could no longer see them. They had already entered into the trees, into the darkness that seemed to Koi-ehm-toya absolute. . . . (pp. 23–24)

I confess that I've felt that way as students weasel their ways and minds out of my control. Yet, I can't twist them into my model. That makes a whole lot of people nervous—administrators, other teachers, parents, along with me and the students. Nonetheless, we find our way through the possibilities of idiosyncratic differences. That doesn't mean we ever agree or carry a shared knowledge away from our work together. It does mean we come to recognize the differences. Maybe we even appreciate them, but I'm not of a predisposition to have my say about how students would tell this same story. So I stand by them mostly and watch how they come to find and define themselves.

The purposes and content of literature education have been vigorously debated. From the traditional canon, with its narrowly defined fundamentals of great books in Western civilization (Bennett, 1984; Bloom, 1987; Hirsch, 1987), to the assertion that the world is rapidly becoming a global village filled with pluralistic perspectives and experiences (Freire, 1971; Shrewbury, 1987; McIntosh, 1981; Winkler, 1986), the legitimacy of whose songs, merriment, and gibes is debated. Is unanimity the desired outcome of such discussions? It seems so when we relinquish our assuredness that learning is idiosyncratic and personal.

As the arguments become higher pitched, teachers often yield to the textbook writers. The literature anthology looms larger than life in most classrooms, shutting out the teacher's and the students' voices from the discussion about whose knowledge is worth knowing.

I'm unmasking my beliefs about the knowledge I've validated in literature classrooms over the years. I'm more mindful that the scope of my inquiry cannot rest complacently on a legitimized knowledge born and nurtured in everyman's tradition. Patience is not one of my virtues. I want to knock down the walls that block my vision of curricular reconstruction. These walls fortify and legitimize the dominant culture in which I've always felt comfortable.

Curriculum is a socially constructed artifact, the intellectual baggage built up over hundreds of years of stasis and change. I haven't taken responsibility for the baffling challenge of cradling curriculum in my hands, questioning it, finding its "infinite jest . . . fancy . . . gibes . . . and songs" to effect changes in practices long established by tradition and experience. As Florence Howe writes, ". . . teaching is a political act: some person is choosing, for whatever reasons, to teach a set of values, ideas, assumptions, and pieces of information, and in so doing, to omit other values, ideas, assumptions, and pieces of information" (1984, p. 282).

John Locke wrestled with similar issues in the questions he asked: Should classics or sciences be the foundation of curriculum? Should formal logic be stressed or the study of mathematics? Should teachers emphasize obedience or freedom? Is general education more important than the development of specific skills?

The teacher as archeologist needs to know the history of education to understand curriculum as artifact. The competing and emerging voices of curriculum continuously shape the social construction of knowledge about teaching and learning. But, we must decide for ourselves, be able to fully articulate and to take a stand on what curriculum is and can be. This requires a long-term commitment to the hard business of inquiry and a willingness not to hold our tongues or energies.

Teacher as Anthropologist

The trick is not to impose my versions of knowledge on students or have someone else impose their versions on me. The hierarchical structures of schools encourage voice and voicelessness by setting up formidable walls across which we cannot speak to one another. Students listen to teachers, teachers listen to principals, principals listen to superintendents, and parents mostly listen to each other, to critics of education, and test results.

Much of this discourages the self-reflexive processes that nurture our work. I mean that. We have this situation where the school day is reduced to mechanistically or numbly performing *900 Shows A Year* as Palonsky (1986) reminds us. Attendance-taking, copy-machine bottle-necks, and outside agendas fill each day with routines and pressures that can keep us from confronting ourselves in serious dialogue about strategies for thinking through and improving our work.

I remember it clearly. The place was in a high school where I'd taught for nearly twenty years. The time was late May in any one of those years ...

I dutifully separated excused absences from the activity, extraordinary, and unexcused ones. That day I found at least seven students absent each hour—cheerleader tryouts, a tennis tournament, the debaters were at Stanford, and at least eight of the Junior Achievement students were at J. C. Penney's 2nd Annual White Sale. Or, I'd become cynical enough to believe or to say it for effect. Student-body officers, the watchdogs of democracy, were at the polling booths for student elections. The campaigns had reached a fervor.

Then a note: "Teachers, Please adjust your schedule tomorrow for a series of assemblies. A–H, 2nd period; I–P, 3rd period; and Q–Z, 4th period." I'd quit asking why.

The clincher. During sixth period, just as Brian was midsentence and headed for his closing lines of a story he'd been working on, a colleague threw open the door to tell me a gas pipe had broken and we were evacuating the building. It wasn't until 4:20, as I made the turn from Capitol Boulevard onto University Drive, that I remembered the principal would be evaluating sixth hour tomorrow. Should I pick up midsentence with Brian? Should I really write my objective on the board? After this day, it would read, scrawled in large letters: SURVIVE UNTIL JUNE.

Grains of my best intentions as a teacher, along with grains of frustration, were slipping through my fingers carrying resolve and energy with them. If I could just close the door and teach . . . if I could just . . .

There is enough of the Puritan ethic in me that I stuck with twenty-three Mays in public school. As each spring neared, my resolve to carefully consider the students and our work together faded further from reality. The classroom neared 100 degrees. A student was admitted to an intervention program for drug and alcohol abuse. I was assigned hall duty when I wasn't administering semester tests. "But," I tried to reason with the powers that be, "all the students are in tests so who is in the hall other than the teachers?" It did no good. I sat patiently, staring at emptiness and quiet. Tired and worn out, I quit asking.

Three computers were down while students were finishing their writing portfolios. James lost his book. Had I seen it? "I know I left it in this room. What did you do with it?" A note from the principal's office: "Someone pulled a fire alarm in your hall. Any ideas?" My note back: "Aren't I supposed to be in my room teaching at 2:15 pm? The fire alarm is, well, maybe not a city block away but close to it."

Then a note from the VP in the Financial Office: "See me immediately. We need a budget for Ski Team." Note back: "Does immediately really mean immediately? I have 36 sophomore boys with May hormones surging. Any suggestions?"

As May wore on, I could hear the wicked stepmother and stepsisters calling: Cinderella! Cinderella! Cinderella! But, the mice did not burst forth with harmonious song to keep me from disintegrating into rages. "Just what is in teachers' hands?" I keep asking.

Some reform literature depicts school culture as static and antiseptic. Profiles of teachers, described through various roles, activities, and stages of effectiveness reflect research done upon teachers. We know better. The ever increasingly pluralistic culture of schools needs careful consideration from those living within it. Like common sense gone transcendental, the culture of schools has been described as devoid of context or color. The voices of those within have not spoken often enough for themselves and have allowed translations of their knowledge to speak in their places. All this fiddling around from the outside-in represents a yawning gap of something being missed: What exactly are the participants in the school culture saying for themselves?

As anthropologist Clifford Geertz (1983) warns,

> Rather than attempting to place the experience of others within the framework of such a conception (of how a person is set against the whole of what people are), which is what the extolled "empathy" in fact usually comes down to, understanding them demands setting that conception aside and seeing their experiences within the framework of their own idea of what selfhood is. (p. 59)

Now, without overstating the issues, anthropology can be of use to us teachers. We might wander the maze of our metaphoric streets and squares, searching out the coffee shops and suburbs that are the cultural life of our schools. This is my desire: to render this world of school distinct and not subject it to prescriptions laid upon it from other cultures.

Sometimes, in this journey, we will not be proud of ourselves. The faculty room, which I'll liken to the Parisian café or smoke-filled English Common Room, may fail to meet our expectations of what we'd anticipated would go on there. Too often the talk is half-examined and shifts from one mundane ritual or frustration to another. If we've taken a detour, we can, as anyone with uncommon sense knows, turn around and face ourselves. We can renovate the place rather than hire an interior decorator who will mask what's really lacking—deliberate and serious talk about how we've mitred, jointed, and polished the culture we've constructed.

We often work in isolation, shut in and off from meaningful dialogue with one another, with ourselves, and the larger school culture. Busyness replaces thoughtfulness in the existing structures of school. And teachers aren't speaking out. We get caught up in the maze and complexity of these structures, come up against dead ends, and search for trap doors as cure-alls that might lead us forward.

But where do we want to be headed? Beyond and behind this, I'd like Geertz to have the last word:

> It is not a new cryptography that we need, especially when it consists of replacing one cipher by another less intelligible, but a new diagnostics, a science that can determine the meaning of things for the life that surrounds them. It will have, of course, to be trained on signification, not pathology, and treat with ideas, not with symptoms. But by connecting incised statues, pigmented sago palms, frescoed walls, and chanted verse to jungle clearing, totem rites, commercial inference, or street argument, it can perhaps begin at last to locate in the tenor of their setting the sources of their spell. (1983, p. 120)

Teacher as Artist

My grandmother, Helen, was a potter, mostly for self-satisfaction. She supplied her ten children with dinner plates, bowls, and goblets long before it became fashionable to have anything other than Haviland in the china cupboard. For me, her potting fired my imagination. I would sit by her side, the moist clay in hand, and fashion, at my will, colonies of imaginary beings—shapes of extraordinary people, demonic animals, or peaceful creatures who roamed the caves, hills, and valleys of civilizations I'd construct in the corner of her garden. Thus, I was occupied day after day and seemingly now, at this great distance, year after year.

I'm aware that it was the feel of clay in my hands as I released form from it that exhilarated me. I named, and maybe I, like Pan-ku or Prometheus, breathed imagination, intellect, and much dissatisfaction into the minds and hearts of these creations.

Not long ago, after my grandmother's death, her dresser was carried to our family home. I opened the bottom drawer—no small drawer in fact—maybe six feet long, two feet high, and three feet deep. In that drawer, carefully wrapped in tissue, sealed with tape long since yellowed and crumbling, arranged in upwards of thirty cigar boxes, were the great actors and actresses of the civilizations I'd fashioned along with the artifacts of their culture—odd buildings, torture devices, and furniture.

Seeing these again, I felt the power of such shaping, the exhilaration of my imaginings, wild and free, that brought life and stories into the long hours of one seven-year-old's days. I lived again those moments. Only the landscape was missing, for the corner of that garden where I'd shaped these worlds had long since given way to the civilizing influence of grass seed.

I was the shaper not only of form but also of culture—albeit a snug and insular one. Now, from my vantage point in the broader currents of the culture that I've been keeping—Wittgenstein, Vygotsky, Gadamer, Frye, Barthes, and Kuhn—my shaping seems small and insignificant. But the experience brought me to think again what teaching is and is not.

To be a teacher is to be part of a constructive and shaping enterprise. Should we mold students in our images? How much of the shaping is in our hands? The story of teaching is a personal story, as personal as the worlds of imaginings I created in clay. Are we student advocates, awakeners of their desire to shape a new culture? Should we nurture them into making their own art? The art of teaching rests on the fulcrum's balancing point—awakening the imaginings on one hand, allowing students the freedom to shift and move in their own directions on the other. Always providing the model of ourselves as artists. The story of teacher as shaper is told over and over again.

For me it began with Miss Elizabeth Melton, fourth grade, Washington School. Reading *Anne of Green Gables, Alice in Wonderland,* or *Black Beauty* to the class after lunch on long spring afternoons, I realized the power of words to create and control imagination. From Miss Melton's class I carried her love of words, of books, and a powerful desire to write. I started writing a novel that year. She held in her hands the power to awaken my sensitivity to language and story. She was part of a long tradition of those who have earned the name teacher.

Take Plato. Plato's allegory of the cave has perennial significance for teachers who take the role of teaching seriously. Plato depicted learning as a journey from the chains of illusion, shadows, and darkness of the cave into a world of enlightenment. So, too, do teachers find the journey arduous. The difficulty is not the lack of content knowledge. That can be cured easily. Nor is it knowing how to plan units, lessons, and activities. That skill develops with experience. It is the willingness to live with uncertainty and understand that learning does not fall neatly into categories, labels, or sequences. Hannah Arendt (1959) pointed out, in her Prologue to *The Human Condition*, that a "heedless

recklessness or helpless confusion or complacent repetition of truths
. . . become trivial and empty" (p. 6). All this is worth wondering about
and questioning.

At times we hold narrowness and impatience in our hands and feel
the need to reshape the clay into new images. At times we hold the
narrow dream of actuality or raw intellect, but shape it into the dream
of wisdom. Buddha taught compassion; Confucius taught tolerance and
respect for a variety of opinions. "Truth cannot be monopolized," he
said. "Propriety; avoidance of extremes, the educated person does not
impose his opinions on others."

The current educational literature is full of studies on reform. Many
grow out of two 1986 reports — Holmes and Carnegie — where increased
professional status and strengthened career-advancement opportunities will cure the ills of education. But will any easy formulaic
approach work? I get nervous by watchwords in education — CORT,
TACTICS, BACK TO BASICS. Each suggests again that all of us can
fit into a mold as teacher or learner and take on, as evening wear,
someone else's costume. Don't we then risk losing the art of being
individual?

Greenberg (1969), in his study of teachers' feelings, noted that we
try to live up to false myths. Roland Barthes (1982) likens the sport of
wrestling to a spectacle equivalent to the solar spectacles of Greek
drama and bullfights (p. 18). I can't help but draw, in equivalent
terms, that metaphor to teaching. When and how is teaching reduced
to a staged performance enacted before spectators (i.e., students, peers,
the principal)? Are the polite, conventional gestures of official rules
and official knowledge what we perpetuate because we don't know how
to do things better? Or, to keep the tranquility? Do the teaching
spectacles create an "exhaustion of the content by the form" (p. 22)?

I've come to realize that I left behind the shaping of one culture for
another. This came as a complete surprise to me when I opened the
drawer again through this story of myself. I have been asked numerous
times why I teach. Perhaps the beginning of my answer starts in the
story I've told — my grandmother, the clay, the garden, and the shaping.
As Grumet (1988) reminds me:

> As we study the forms of our own experience we are not searching
> only for evidence of the external forces that have diminished us;
> instead, we are recovering our own possibilities, ways of knowing and
> being in the world that we remember and imagine and must draw
> into language that can span the chasm that presently separates what
> we know as our public and private worlds. (p. 532)

Small stories. Personal stories. Indeed, these reveal who I am as teacher, where I've come from, and where I may be going. Through them I might construct definitions of myself as teacher. Carolyn Steedman (1986) in *Landscape for a Good Woman* reflects that "... the compulsions of narrative are almost irresistible" (p. 144). I think our stories are worth telling if only to testify to ourselves that, as Eudora Welty (1983) tells us, "a light is thrown back, as when your train makes a curve, showing that there has been a mountain of meaning rising behind you on the way you've come ... proven through retrospect" (p. 90). And so on.

Teacher as Reformer

Maybe I've suggested too frequently that we must wander the labyrinth of intentions and meanings, search for ourselves only to get lost again. I think that's a way toward change. Education is particularly prey to the "quick fix." Rousseau warned that

> When I see a man carried away by his love for knowledge, hastening from one alluring science to another without knowing where to stop, I think I see a child gathering shells upon a seashore. At first he loads himself with them; then, tempted by others he throws these away, and gathers more. At last, weighed down by so many, and no longer knowing which to choose, he ends by throwing all away, and returning empty-handed.

Are we to be left with nothing but our grumblings when we are asked to swallow pills we gag on? How will the dust jacket read on the history of education book that will be written on these years around the turn of another century? Will it tell of a turf war too great? One that brought the battle to an end much where it had started? Raising these questions challenges us to consciously and consistently consider the issues. The point is: I think the dialogue must include those in the school culture, those who nurture new ideas and new learning. It will necessitate that teachers take an active and informed role in the dialogue.

The question for American education will be whether in diversity we can enter genuine dialogue that will help us make the important decisions in an ever-changing educational culture. There is no Wizard of Oz at the end of the educational yellow brick road. Remember, he turned out to be a fraud anyway. It may have been the journey itself, the constant living with danger, speculation, learning, and sharing that had meaning to Dorothy and her companions. For me it has indeed been the journey.

Therefore, I would like to end where, as a teacher, I became interested in teaching, learning, and thinking. There is a long accounting of students with whom I shared a brief moment — Sarah Benedict, Tim Oakes, Marshall High, Susan Stradler, Scott Smith, Ted Faulkner, and Susan Fowler. Perhaps a hundred remember the day in class when we shed a tear together for Tess of the D'Urbervilles and for our own humanity. Six may remember that Othello killed Desdemona. All will know that revenge and greed as well as charity and forgiveness have consequences. Nowhere in the history of education could another teacher construct this same list of names that sums up what was partially in my hands.

They're with me still. Otherwise, how can I hear Scott's voice or the full pealing laughter of Ted before drugs or remember lines from Mark Lindholm's "Michael Flaherty" revenge piece? "Michael Flaherty runs like a girl. His strides are too short. His arms flail at his sides like he's swatting at mosquitos. . . ." How can I remember Sarah's description of her grandfather kneading the bellies of salmon? "A thousand eggs were fertilized, sent back into the waters where the river doesn't roar. He had two purposes in the last of his life: to fish and to keep the river populated. In a way it's like a hand from God, something natural and unnatural at the same time."

It isn't memory. It's having been an aerial for ideas, awakenings, and imaginings. Drawing those students into themselves and through themselves somehow drew them right through the marrow of me.

We must keep the learning. That's what we have in our hands — the responsibility to do just that.

REFERENCES

Arendt, H. (1959). *The human condition*. New York: Anchor Books.

Barthes, R. (1982). *A Barthes reader*. S. Sontag (Ed.). New York: Hill and Wang.

Bennet, W. J. (1984). *To reclaim a legacy*. Washington, DC: National Endowment for the Humanities.

Bloom, A. (1987). *The closing of the American mind*. New York: Simon & Schuster.

Boyer, E. L. (1983). *High school*. New York: Harper and Row.

Freire, P. (1971). *Pedagogy of the oppressed*. New York: Herder and Herder.

Geertz, C. (1983). *Local knowledge*. New York: Basic Books.

Goodlad, J. I. (1984). *A place called school: Prospects for the future*. New York: McGraw-Hill.

Greenberg, H. (1969). *Teaching with feeling: Compassion and self-awareness in the classroom today*. New York: Macmillan.

Grumet, M. (1988). *Bitter Milk: Women and Teaching*. Amherst: University of Massachusetts Press.

Hirsch, E. D. Jr. (1987). *Cultural literacy*. Boston: Houghton Mifflin.

Howe, F. (1984). *Myths of coeducation*. Bloomington: Indiana University Press.

McIntosh, P. (1981). The study of women: Implications for reconstructing the liberal arts discipline. *The Forum For Liberal Education* 4(1), 1−3.

Momaday, N. S. (1989). *Ancient child*. New York: Harpers.

Palnosky, S. B. (1986). *900 shows a year: A look at teaching from a teacher's side of the desk*. New York: Random House.

Rousseau, J. J. (1760). *Emile*. London: J. M. Dent & Sons, 1957.

Shrewbury, C. M. (1987). What is feminist pedagogy? *Women's Studies Quarterly* 15 (3 & 4), 6−13.

Steedman, C. (1986). *Landscape for a good woman: A story of two lives*. London: Virago Press.

Welty, E. (1983). *One writer's beginnings*. Cambridge, MA: Harvard University Press.

Winkler, K. (1986, July 9). Flourishing research in Marxist theory belies signs of its demise, scholars say. *Chronicle of Higher Education*, 4−5.

Notes on Contributors

Bob Beichner is keeping busy watching kids learn with the help of computers. The rest of his time is spent helping prospective educators make the switch from student to teacher and back again.

Diane Brunner is currently working on a book that uses stories of schooling in film and literature to dramatize classroom situations. Having come from a family of storytellers, she naturally relies on the power of stories in her work. She believes in the inherent ability of narrative to connect art with life to help us make sense of our world. "Stories draw us into their worlds; there our experiences help us reflect on the past to plan for the future."

Jim Collins has an English-teaching daughter who, after a recent drastic haircut, read this on the homework paper of one of her students: "Your hair looks great. To change is to live." Jim enjoys running and eating and finds they go well together, just like teaching and learning.

Denise David more and more finds herself pushing aside her teacher's desk and settling in with her students as a fellow reader, writer, and learner. "My classroom has become a place where I can learn to teach better. From closely watching and listening to my students, I have begun to confront some of the tough questions that have floated just under the surface for as long as I have been teaching."

The English teachers of Rockdale County, Georgia were as traditional a bunch as you could find a year ago. No more! Some credit for their success with restructuring goes to supportive administrators who allowed and encouraged them to grow. Most credit, however, goes to their own willingness to trust intuitions developed over many years as dedicated, caring professionals.

Carolyn Handa teaches at American River College in Sacramento, California. She has edited a collection of essays entitled *Computers and Community:*

Teaching Composition in the Twenty-first Century for Boynton/Cook. She has also published assorted essays on the poetry of Elizabeth Bishop.

Harriet Malinowitz is currently writing her dissertation (which emerged from the chapter in this volume) at New York University, and is also at work on her second play, which is based on oral histories with three older Jewish lesbians. She is interested in the ways that activism, art, and academia spill over into one another. She hopes that lesbian and gay studies programs will soon begin to proliferate on campuses across the country, and that one day she will teach in one.

Suzanne Miller has learned through years of high school teaching and re-search that students involved regularly in genuine discussion see themselves as thinkers. Her favorite evidence of this comes from Sam, an urban eleventh-grader, who said, "After class I have discussions in my mind, so it's hard to concentrate in gym class." Suzanne hopes more teachers will try new ways of talking in classrooms. "In supported discussions students can learn to form questions, shape meaning, and sustain inquiry in words that speak as loudly as other actions."

Deborah Mutnick directs the Writing Center at Long Island University in Brooklyn, where she learns a lot about what goes on both in the inner city and in writing classes. As a teacher, she would like to promote student writing as a valuable source of knowledge about the world. "Students have something important to say, given the chance. I think we teachers ought to stop talking so much and learn to listen more."

Susan Ohanian is married to a physicist who volunteered to teach first-year composition to science majors as part of a college restructuring effort to spread this course across curricular departments. He withdrew his offer when the English faculty insisted that, no matter who taught the course, every student had to read *Gulliver's Travels* and Plato's *Republic.*

Sally Hudson-Ross felt something like Tom Wolfe recording the progress of that 1960s magical bus in writing her chapter. Some may say that Sally had something to do with the acceptance of restructuring by the English teachers of Rockdale County, Georgia, but she claims she simply had the honor of going along for the ride.

David Schaafsma thinks of himself primarily as a storyteller. Some of his stories are published as "Short Stories," and he sees classroom research itself as a form of storytelling, but most of his stories are shared through his teaching in the classroom. A former high school English teacher, he was a teacher in and director of the Dewey Center Community Writing Project in